The Cleanse Cookbook

Christine's Cleanse Corner
P.O. Box 28895, San Diego, CA 92198
Info: (858) 673-0224
Orders: Toll Free (877) 673-0224
www.TransformYourHealth.com

by Christine Dreher, C.C.N, C.C.H.

Published by Christine's Cleanse Corner
P.O. Box 421423
San Diego, CA 92142
www.TransformYourHealth.com

Design and production by Alan Chmielewski,
Gemini Services, San Diego, CA
www.GeminiServices.com

Edited by Brenda Noonan
www.Trailgator-tech.com

Suggestions and ideas presented in this book are for information only and should not be interpreted as medical advice. The author recommends that readers consult their health care provider before beginning any cleanse, diet or detoxification program.

ISBN 0-9658687-7-X

First Edition, March, 1997
First Printing, March, 1997
Second Printing, February, 1998
Third Printing, May, 2001

Printed in the U.S.A.

Foreword

I have had the privilege of knowing Christine Dreher since 1995 – she is truly an inspiring example of personal transformation and the cleansing lifestyle. I see her as one of the leaders in the field of cleansing and transformation in this new millennium. Her continual dedication to helping others obtain health, healing and wellness is admirable. Her motivational lectures and her sharing of the benefits of cleansing are contagious! These qualities also shine true in her book, "The Cleanse Cookbook." This book is an outstanding compilation of cleanse-worthy recipes and cleanse information put together in a "user friendly" fashion that helps cleansers succeed during and after their cleanse programs. It is also a helpful guide for those wanting to transition to a healthier diet and lifestyle, as well as those wanting to work on pH balance or on allergy-restricted diets. I encourage all of you to continue to take your next steps toward "Radiant Health and Energy" and to be an inspiration and example for others.

Sincerely,

Richard Anderson, ND, NMD,
author of "Cleanse & Purify Thyself 1 & 2",
Arise & Shine Herbal Products Founder

Foreword

About *The Cleanse Cookbook*

The Cleanse Cookbook is a one-of-a-kind cleanse resource guide. It provides a variety of delicious and creative cleanse recipes, as well as valuable information on vegetables, grains, organic food and natural seasonings. It also includes food preparation tips, information on the internal body cleansing process, importance of pH balance, pH testing methods and much more.

The Cleanse Cookbook was created to support and assist cleansers through their cleanse and detoxification programs and to educate them on the value of cleansing and balancing their pH levels. This book provides healthy alkaline-forming cleanse recipes that help to balance the body's pH level and encourage the body to detoxify and clean out. It can be used with a cleanse program or is effective to use by itself to assist in balancing the pH levels of the body.

Many people are toxic due in part to eating too many processed, acid-forming foods that create congestion and depletion of essential nutrients in the body. This can result in imbalanced pH levels, compromised body functions and eventually dis-ease. By restoring the body's pH balance and electrolyte minerals, the body can respond naturally and begin the cleansing and healing process – creating health and harmony, instead of toxicity and disease.

The Cleanse Cookbook is also a helpful tool for people with allergies or restricted diets because it contains no sugar, salt, wheat, dairy, meat, gluten or yeast.

About the Author

Christine Dreher is a Clinical Nutritionist, Clinical Herbalist and Cleanse Coach. She is the owner of Christine's Cleanse Corner, a cleanse company dedicated to helping cleansers with information, support, cleanse resources and products to "Clean Out and Feel Better." She is a cleanse lecturer and teacher, motivational speaker and workshop leader. Her own cleansing transformation inspires her to continue helping thousands of cleansers worldwide. The following is Christine's story into the journey of cleansing and transformation.

The Cleanse Cookbook was inspired by my first 40-day intestinal cleanse process that transformed my life in so many incredible ways. I completed my first cleanse over seven years ago. Prior to this time, I had undergone years of "purging and healing of emotions, mind and spirit" and now my body was ready to catch up, release, heal and transform. Within the first week of the cleanse, I had already noticed dramatic results. My complexion cleared, my eyes became whiter and brighter, and the puffiness in my face disappeared. I felt lighter, and my weight began dropping. As I continued the cleanse, I lost over 35 pounds and have maintained my ideal weight since. I also noticed more energy and vitality. Also, the constipation and abdominal bloating went away. I not only cleansed my physical body, I also continued to clear away old emotional and mental baggage stored in my body. My attitude about life became more positive and my self-image improved immensely. The more I cleansed, the more I detoxified. I felt so much lighter, like a whole new person!

Others around me were amazed at my incredible and very noticeable transformation. Many of them also wanted to cleanse. I left my accounting career behind and entered the world of cleansing. I studied nutrition and herbs and trained as a cleanse coach. More and more people were coming to me for cleansing and my cleanse business was born! As I continued to coach and help many cleansers through their cleanse programs, I was constantly asked for help with cleanse foods and pH information. I discovered there was a need for a cleanse book guide to support cleansers during and after their cleanse processes.

I am an intuitive lover of cooking and it has always been exciting for me to create new, healthy dishes. So I got to work and compiled my cleanse recipes and information together. I contacted many cleanse customers who also enjoyed cooking and asked them for their favorite cleanse recipes. I also contacted two chef friends who had cleansed with me. I asked them to contribute their cleanse recipes. And so, the creation of *The Cleanse Cookbook*.

I am excited to share this cleanse information with you. I invite you to contact me to share your comments, suggestions, questions or recipes for future editions.

If you would like to know more about the 40-day cleanse process that helped me so much, I recommend reading *Cleanse & Purify Thyself 1.0 and 2.0* and *the Cleanse Program Guide* by Dr. Rich Anderson. See "Cleanse Information" in the Resource section in the back of this book.

My commitment to you and the world is to support all levels of healing and transformation, including physical, emotional, mental, and spiritual; to support us in becoming all that we Truly are, letting go of all the "baggage, toxins, illusions, etc.," that hold us back. To your Health, Well-being, and Freedom!

♥ Christine Dreher ♥

Acknowledgments

I would like to thank the following people for their contributions.

The two chefs were:

Sharna Gross, Marin County, CA. - Sharna began her career at 17 years old with her own catering business. She graduated from the California Culinary Academy in San Francisco, CA. Her expertise in cooking came from restaurants in the San Francisco Bay area, including: Domain Chandon, a classical French kitchen; Stars Restaurant; running and operating Stars Cafe, and Ozone. In Santa Fe, New Mexico, she worked with Santa Cafe and Coyote Cafe. She has been a consultant for many restaurants, helping them with menu and recipe development. Sharna's recipe creations during her cleanse were remarkable.

Ivi Turner, San Diego, CA. - Ivi has her own catering business and many years of cooking experience. Her love and knowledge of food and nutrition, combined with the balance of textures, colors, and flavors is outstanding. Her recipes have been tested on very discriminating children, as well as the gourmet palates of adults.

Thanks to Jamey Dina, N.D. and Kim Sproul, N.D., Escondido, CA, for their recipe contributions from their wonderful cookbook _Uncooking with Jamey & Kim_. I attended one of their "Uncooking" workshops and loved it. The food was absolutely delicious!

Thanks to Phyllis Avery for her "Juicing" contribution from her wonderful book, *The Garden of Eden Raw Fruit and Vegetable Recipes*.

A special thanks to the following cleansers and friends for their recipe contributions:

Andrew & Kathleen Myler, Los Angeles, CA
Angela Green, Boulder, CO
Dan Napier, Chef, San Diego, CA
Emily Mudhur Fung, Blackheath, London, England
Estelle Russom, New Kirk, OK
Jaque Frank, Hudson, FL
Jessica Frank, Hudson, FL
Jessie Ann, Chino Valley, AZ
Laura Sellens, Missoula, MT
Mary Jane Heinrichs, Lincoln, NE
Michael Goggins, Missoula, MT
Molly Wieler, Boulder, CO
Peter Dyke, San Diego, CA
Sharon Skylor, Mill Valley, CA
Sherry Baquial, San Diego, CA
Xanthe Skjelfjord, Charlottesville, VA

I would like to acknowledge Dr. Rich Anderson, a brilliant pioneer and inspiring visionary in the world of natural healing and cleansing, the creator of the Arise and Shine Cleanse program, and the author of *Cleanse & Purify Thyself*. Also, thanks to Dr. Bernard Jensen for his extensive knowledge regarding the internal cleansing process.

And a very special thanks to Alan Chmielewski, my co-publisher, design consultant, and coach for this book. He saw me through this whole process with so much love, support, patience, and hard work.

DEDICATION

I dedicate this book to the countless people who have touched my life, my heart, and my soul so deeply. To you all, I am grateful.

A special dedication of love and gratitude to all the angels with "Amanae," "Frequencies of Brilliance," and "Miracle of Love," disguised as people.

To my late grandfather, Ted "Rube" Dreher, who saw me through some very tough times with so much humor, love, understanding, and support.

To Alan Chmielewski, a very special gift from God, a dear soulmate, sweetheart, and true friend; you stand with me in love, honesty, integrity, trust, and truth. Lovingly, you encourage me to open, trust, love, heal, stay present, and let go of the past.

"The doctor of the future will give no medicine, but will interest his patients in the care of the human frame, in diet, and in the cause and prevention of disease."

Thomas Edison

Contents

Contents

Contents

Contents

Sauces and Dips 177

Desserts 199

Contents

Introduction

Introduction

What Is Cleansing?

Most people spend so much time and effort cleaning their external environment, i.e., their bodies, clothes, houses, cars, etc., but do not spend enough or any time cleaning their internal environment, i.e., their blood, intestines, kidneys, lungs, liver, etc. With the evolution of modern society, the internal body is being stressed more than ever before, overloaded with chemicals, toxins, air pollution, and radiation. Not to mention the toxins we ingest through our mouths: the processed and de-mineralized foods, herbicides, pesticides, food colorings, preservatives, and greasy, acid-based foods. These poisons can cause excessive stress on the entire physiology of our bodies, weakening our immune systems, digestive systems, and eliminative organs. Once these systems are weakened, the other glands and organs become weakened and stressed, resulting in chronic and degenerative diseases.

When our bodies are clean and healthy, it is easier to eliminate toxins. But when our bodies become overloaded with toxins, they become sluggish and more susceptible to disease because the immune system no longer has the capability of fighting off invading diseases. Then, when the body manifests discomfort and symptoms of imbalance (headaches, indigestion, gas, fatigue, aches and pains, just to name a few), most people try to cover up the symptoms or cure them with more chemicals, instead of seeking the cause of the system imbalance. As the first trouble indicators are often suppressed or ignored, the body's signals eventually become louder, resulting in more serious health problems due to the continuous overload of toxicity in the body. Not to mention the repressed and denied emotions and mental stress that also take their toll on the health of the body. Eventually, when the system

Introduction

becomes stagnant and can no longer rid itself of toxins, chronic disease or death manifests.

Effective cleansing and body detoxification are the keys to a healthy, balanced system. By eliminating the toxic accumulation, the causes of many health problems are also eliminated. The body is then able to fight off infections and bacterial invasions more efficiently. According to Dr. Bernard Jensen, "It is the bowel that invariably has to be cared for first, before effective healing can take place."

Furthermore, the body cannot properly absorb nutrients, vitamins, and health supplements if it is congested and toxic. An analogy would be: putting new oil in a car without draining out the old, dirty oil first. By draining out the old oil first, then adding the new, the car will run better and the engine will run more smoothly. According to Dr. Bernard Jensen, "Every tissue is fed by the blood, which is supplied by the bowel. When the bowel is dirty, the blood is dirty." Before spending time and money consuming quality natural food products and nutritional supplements, the body first needs to rid itself of toxins and encumbering waste material. It is simple. Detoxify and then rebuild properly.

The cleanse philosophy is based on detoxifying the system by removing unwanted materials that cause disease, rather than the ingestion of products that simply treat the symptoms. Internal body cleansing is the most effective way of removing toxins and unwanted waste materials from the body. It is the natural way to detoxify, nourish, and strengthen the body. Not only is it highly effective in cleansing the colon, small intestines, and stomach, it also cleanses at the deep tissue levels. The blood, lymph, liver, kidneys, heart, lungs, skin, and practically every organ and gland are relieved of toxic accumulations.

For more information about cleansing, see the Resources and References section.

I recommend that you consult your health care provider before beginning any cleanse, diet, or detoxification program.

Based on my own cleanse and detoxification experiences, I recommend that you pace yourself. Do not be too extreme in your cleanse and detoxification process. I believe that the body responds better to step-by-step gradual changes rather than sudden abrupt changes. During the cleanse and detoxification process, the body is ridding itself of a lot of toxins that have most likely been accumulating for many years. The process could become extremely uncomfortable or intolerable if done too fast. Balance, moderation, and persistence are the key to successful cleansing and detoxification. Go for it! The endeavor is well worth the effort.

Introduction

Levels of Cleansing

I have discovered that there are many levels of cleansing that can happen during the internal cleanse and detoxification process. The releasing of toxins and the healing of the physical body are the most obvious levels of cleansing. Many of my cleanse customers and I have experienced healing on the emotional, mental, and spiritual levels as well.

During my first 40-day cleanse program, I re-experienced many old memories, feelings, and sensations. Sometimes it was a passing thought, other times it was a memory with a feeling attached. I even experienced sensations and vague memories of my tonsillectomy at 10 years old. Some of these experiences were pleasant and some were not. I perceived these experiences to be repressed and stored at a cellular level in my body.

As I cleansed my physical body, I also seemed to cleanse my mind, emotions, and entire being simultaneously. I felt lighter as the cleanse process went on. My energy increased, my attitude became more positive, and my self-image improved. I let go of a lot of old emotional "stuff" that I no longer needed. It felt like a purging of my mind, body, emotions, and entire being. I call this "spiritual healing and transformation" because it includes the entire being, not just the physical body.

Growing up as the oldest of 5 children in a very dysfunctional family environment, I was not allowed to express any dissension, pain, anger, or frustration. I was taught, by example, to stuff these feelings down, by covering them with "comfort foods" (foods that tend to alter moods, such as sugar, chocolate, caffeine, pastries, ice cream, etc.). As I started letting go of my attachment to these comfort foods during my cleanse process, old memories, sensations, and feelings began to emerge into my consciousness – experiences that I perceived as having been stuffed down with comfort foods years before. I allowed these suppressed experiences to surface. I fully experienced them, resulting in healing, release, completion, and a feeling of freedom.

Since my first cleanse, I have continued to do a great deal of cleansing, releasing, and healing on all levels of my being. I have found this process to be truly transforming. I feel better than ever before about myself and others. I am finding peace, joy, love, and even ecstasy inside myself. I believe these qualities are our natural state and we only need to uncover ourselves from all the layers of "stuff" to find our true, harmonious, and loving nature. I see it as sort of a treasure hunt inside ourselves. I believe the most valuable treasures are all buried within.

For more information about spiritual healing and transformation, see the Resources and References section.

Introduction

The Importance of a Balanced pH

One of the purposes of *The Cleanse Cookbook* is to educate the public about the importance of a balanced pH level in the body. The book focuses primarily on alkaline pH foods for two reasons:

- The average American diet is far too acidic, which creates serious imbalances, toxicity, and congestion in the body.

- During the cleanse and detoxification process it is important to greatly reduce or eliminate acid-forming foods because they create more congestion and mucus in the body and slow down the cleanse process.

What is a balanced pH? The pH level is measured on a scale of 0 to 14. The midpoint, 7, is considered to be neutral; above 7 is alkaline and below 7 is acidic. The higher the number, the more alkaline; the lower the number, the more acidic.

The pH level varies in different areas of the body. For example, the pH of the blood should be at 7.4, whereas the pH of stomach (gastric) juices range from 1.0 to 3.5. The small intestines need an alkaline environment of 7.0 or higher for the various enzymes of the intestine to function properly and for proper assimilation of nutrients. If the small intestines are too acidic, then the enzymes can not function. This can create bacterial disturbances, congestion, and a breakdown of the intestinal lining. An overly acidic environment in the intestines can create various symptoms, including gas, constipation, diarrhea, bloating, colon irritation, and disease.

Introduction

The following information is reprinted with permission from the author, Dr. Rich Anderson, from his book *Cleanse & Purify Thyself.*

Understanding pH the Acid/Alkaline Balance

Every breath we take and even the beating of our hearts depend upon our bodies maintaining a precisely balanced pH in the blood, and in other critical body elements. Every enzyme system in the body is influenced by pH. This means that without proper pH, cells cannot receive the nutrients and energy they need to stay healthy. As cells weaken, they cannot perform well. If this persists, tissues and whole organs begin to malfunction. This then impairs the functioning of whole body systems, and serious disease begins to evolve.

Excluding accidents and genetic weakness, disease most often begins to occur after we have altered our normal pH balance by becoming deficient in minerals, especially electrolyte minerals, not minerals from rock, but minerals from organic matter (plants). The body cannot efficiently use rock minerals. It must use the minerals that have passed throughout the plant kingdom. Minerals from the plant kingdom are rock minerals that have been chelated to a protein molecule by the process of photosynthesis.

Anytime our pH is off balance even to a small degree, it is usually a sign that we have depleted ourselves of valuable electrolyte minerals. An electrolyte is any compound that, in solution, conducts electricity, and is decomposed by it. Sodium, potassium, calcium, magnesium, lithium and phosphorus are the primary electrolytes that the body needs. A lack of organic minerals anywhere in our bodies means a decrease in enzyme function, and a corresponding deterioration in cell health. When this occurs, many of our organs and glands may be under great stress, for only slight changes in pH from normal levels can cause extreme alterations in the rates of chemical reactions inside and outside the cells. Some cells will be depressed; others

Introduction

will be accelerated. This is why the regulation of pH is one of the
most important physiological functions in maintaining
homeostasis.

When people become too acidotic they are likely to die in a coma,
and when they become too alkalotic they are likely to die of
tetany or convulsions. At a certain point between the two, we
have health, but if the pH of any organ or cell moves toward one
of these extremes, dysfunction is always the result. Most people
in America have already lost this delicate balance and are
moving towards these extremes. However, long before they come
close to death, they usually have contracted various disease
conditions which most people are totally unaware of until the
disease has advanced into pain, tiredness, or some other
symptom.

The standard American diet places heavy emphasis on acid-
forming foods. These foods force our bodies to use precious
electrolyte reserves to balance the excess acidity they create. As
long as adequate mineral reserves are present, health is
maintained. However once the reserves are depleted, acid-
forming foods destroy the body's delicate pH balance resulting
in poor function.

Digestion and pH

The main cause of mineral depletion in the Western world today
is the consumption of acid-forming foods. If we eat a diet high in
acid-forming foods, we can become deficient in many minerals
including sodium, calcium, magnesium and potassium. These
four minerals are the most important, for they have a direct
impact upon maintaining proper pH, fluid viscosity, tissue
softness, cell function, and bowel chemistry. An exact pH is
necessary for blood purity, enzyme activity, and full immune
potential.

The further we deplete our minerals and move towards greater
acidity, the more our bodies lose control over pH, the more the

immune system, the liver and all organs are impaired, and the easier it is for various bacteria, viruses, fungus, yeasts, and perhaps protozoa to thrive. From this depletion of minerals and development of acidity, our immune system becomes depressed, we can lose the ability to create hydrochloric acid, the bile turns acid , our normal friendly bacteria mutates, and we may become susceptible to infiltration of "germs." Minerals are essential in maintaining this delicate pH and metabolic balance. In summary, we can lose this balance as a result of: 1) taking drugs (medicinal), which can cause metabolic stress, 2) being stressed, for emotional stress drains us of electrolytes (just as if we were eating acid-forming foods), or 3) eating acid forming foods. In the Western world all three are prevalent; the latter two are the most common.

When we eat, we chew the food and it goes into the stomach. Here it is saturated by hydrochloric acid (HCL) which activates pepsinogen enzymes. The result being a proteolytic enzyme known as active pepsin. This enzyme helps digest protein. It is important to remember that all foods, except oils, have protein. When the stomach has completed its job, it releases the entire mass through the pyloric valve and the food, now very acid from the HCL, enters the duodenum. Here it is saturated by large amounts of alkaline fluids from the Brunner glands, bile, and pancreatic juices. This is absolutely essential, for the pancreatic enzymes can only function optimally in a pH above 7.0. And not only that; before the body can absorb the food into the blood stream and use it, it must bring it up to a 7.4 pH. How does it do this?

Keep in mind that it is very essential for our bodies to maintain a perfect pH balance. As long as our bodies are able to do so, we have a very good chance of maintaining health all through our lives. But if this balance is lost, it is impossible to maintain good health. My estimate is that more than 90% of the American population has lost this balance.

Introduction

Our bodies have several incredible control mechanisms to maintain this delicate balance of pH. One process is called the buffer system or the regulation of acid-base balance. To eliminate complex explanations, we can say that the first step is for the body to buffer the acids by absorbing the acid with sodium bicarbonate. Each time an acid is buffered by the sodium, the pH rises. In this process, the body brings the acids to a level in which it can safely remove them out of the body through the kidneys and increase the pH of the food so that it can be assimilated.

This may bring more clarity . When we eat alkaline-forming foods, there are more than enough electrolytes to buffer whatever acids were in the food and the remainder is an excess of electrolytes. When we eat acid-forming foods, there are not enough electrolytes to buffer the acids and what remains is an excess of acids or a depletion of electrolytes. The body then has to deplete its own alkaline reserves (also needed for exercise, illness and stress) to handle these acids.

If the blood pH begins to drop, and the alkaline mineral supply is depleted, then the body is forced to extract the needed minerals from various organs in the body. For example, if the body removes sodium (the body cannot use sodium chloride, also known as table salt or sea salt, as it is inorganic...and drains organic sodium from our tissues) from the stomach, then the stomach can no longer create hydrochloric acid, used for digestion. If it removes sodium from the bile, then the bile turns acid, which can result in the formation of muquoid plaque in the intestines, as well as creating serious bowel diseases, such as cancer, colitis, etc. If the body robs potassium from the heart, then heart disease may develop. If it robs minerals from the liver, then hundreds of problems can occur, including cancer. If removes minerals from the bones, then osteoporosis and arthritis may occur.

With just about every case of chronic or degenerative disease, the mineral supply has become deficient and the pH of body fluids abnormal. Adequate healing cannot occur until we have replenished our mineral supply and brought our bodies into the proper pH level. The good news is that if we haven't drained ourselves too seriously, then it is easy to rebuild our supplies of electrolyte minerals. Doing pH tests will indicate just how serious these depletions have become...

The following are ways to build our mineral reserves and maintain better health: eat wholesome organically grown fruits and vegetables, cleanse and purify the entire body, rebuild the digestive system and other organs, avoid drugs and other toxins, get plenty of rest and exercise, breathe deeply, and eliminate excessive stress...

For more information about balancing the pH and internal body cleansing, I highly recommend reading Dr. Rich Anderson's book *Cleanse & Purify Thyself*. See the Resources and References section.

Introduction

How to Test Your pH Level

There are many factors that affect pH levels. Eating acidic foods, high stress levels, extreme exercise, and shallow breathing will all cause one's pH level to become more acidic. Because pH readings can vary due to diet and stress levels, I suggest creating a baseline chart of your pH readings. Take them every day, at about the same time of day, for at least a month. The best time of the day to test pH levels is the first thing in the morning before eating or drinking anything.

There are three pH tests I recommend for measuring your pH level: the saliva test, the lemon test, or the urine test.

According to Sam Graci and Harvey Diamond, in their book *The Power of Superfoods* (see the Resources and References section), "saliva pH changes slowly and indicates the alkalizing or acidifying effect of foods you have eaten and your stress load over the past five days. In contrast, urine pH changes rapidly depending on your life stresses and on the foods you have eaten over the past 12 hours." You can use one test, or a combination of tests. I recommend using all three tests (saliva, lemon, and urine) to establish a more accurate baseline.

You will need:

- pH papers (pHydrion papers work well), which can be purchased at most health food stores, drug stores or from your cleanse distributor.

- Pen & Paper

- 1/2 Fresh Lemon, cut in half

Saliva Test:
This test should be performed first thing in the morning on an empty stomach. No food should be eaten for at least two hours before the test. I also suggest not putting anything in your mouth other than water two hours before, because some juices, sugars, and toothpaste may affect the results of the test.

Expel a small sample of saliva into a teaspoon, so that you do not put the chemicals of the paper into your mouth. Tear off a small piece of pH paper and wet it thoroughly in the saliva for several seconds. Compare the color of the wet pH paper to the color chart provided with the pH papers. The pH in the mouth should be in a range of 6.4 to 7.0 (closer to 7.0 is better).

Urine Test:
There are two different testing methods that I recommend. The first method is the easiest. This test is recommended by Sam Graci and Harvey Diamond in their book *The Power of Superfoods* (see the Resources and References section). Collect the first urine sample in the morning, six hours after uninterrupted sleep, in midstream, before drinking or eating anything. Collect other samples two hours after a meal. Place the pH paper in the urine and immediately compare the color of the paper to the color chart.

The ideal range they mention for the first morning reading is 6.8. They state that typically, urine pH levels fluctuate throughout the day as follows: 6.6 to 7.0 at 7:00 a.m., 6.8 to 7.2 at 3:00 p.m., and 7.0 to 7.4 at 9:00 p.m.

The second testing method is recommended by Dr. Rich Anderson in his cleanse guide, *The Arise & Shine Cleanse Thyself Program Guide* (see the Resources and References section). He recommends devoting a day to eating only

Introduction

vegetables and their juices (alkaline-forming foods). The next morning, collect the first urine sample and wet the pH paper. Again, use the color chart to determine your pH level.

The ideal range for this test is 7.0 or higher, indicating your body has a good supply of alkaline minerals and is eliminating the excess through the urine.

6.5 to 6.9 indicates some depletion of alkaline minerals, though not serious.

5.6 to 6.4 indicates depletion of alkaline minerals that is more serious. It is suggested to replenish your alkaline reserves by eating a diet rich in alkaline-forming foods.

5.6 or below indicates that the body is very depleted and has no alkaline reserves. Replenish your alkaline reserves before attempting any cleanse program.

Note: While on a cleansing program and diet, the body can release acid by-products and toxins through the urine. So it is best to check urine pH levels before and after cleansing.

Lemon Test:
This test is recommended by Dr. Rich Anderson from the same program guide as the urine test. This test can be done right after the saliva test. Eat no food for at least two hours before the pH reading. Cut and squeeze the juice of one half lemon into two ounces of water. Swallow the liquid, swishing it in your mouth a little as you swallow. Wait 60 seconds after swallowing, then check your saliva with the pH papers. Record your results and repeat in 60 seconds. Repeat this every 60 seconds for a total of 6 times. Record each result.

If your pH is 7.5 or higher this is a positive health indicator. Your liver has adequate electrolyte (alkaline) reserves.

7.0 to 7.4 indicates you have some alkaline mineral reserves, but not as much as you need. Work on increasing your reserves.

6.9 or below indicates a possible serious condition; the electrolyte (alkaline) reserves are very low and the liver and digestion could be affected.

pH Testing Tips
The best time to take your pH readings is first thing in the morning before eating or drinking anything and before you brush your teeth. Be sure to compare the color of the pH paper as soon as you wet the paper, do not wait to see if the paper continues to darken. If you prefer, for the saliva test, you can spit into a clean cup instead of putting the pH papers against your tongue. For the pH tests, I recommend using the pH Hydrion papers, #067 (range 5.5 to 8.0). These can be obtained at your local health store, from your local cleanse distributor or from me (see the Resource Section).

Both cleansing and replenishing electrolytes can help balance pH levels. The Vegetable Stock recipe (also known as the Potassium Broth) is helpful, as well as alkaline-forming foods, fresh vegetable juices and Super Green foods.

I also recommend testing your pH level on a regular basis to determine how healthy and balanced your system is. For more information about pH levels, see the Resources and References section.

Introduction

Transitioning Away from the S.A.D. (the Standard American Diet)

The SAD diet and lifestyle can cause or contribute to a wide variety of health problems. For many "want-to-be" cleansers, the challenge and transition can be tough. Here are some tips and suggestions to make the transition easier and to prepare for cleansing.

Microwave
Unplug it and use it to store your herbs, teas or vitamins. By disconnecting your microwave, you are not tempted to eat the "processed, frozen, fast foods" from the grocery store that usually have more artificial ingredients than nutrients.

Food Shopping
The best rule of thumb is to do most, if not all, of your shopping on the two outermost aisles of the store. In most stores, this is where you will find the whole foods and produce.

Organic Foods
Buy organic whenever possible, or at least buy pesticide-free produce. If you eat meat and dairy, buy hormone-free and chemical-free poultry, meats and dairy products. These products are usually available at health food stores. By buying organic, you are also freeing yourself of most genetically modified foods. If you can't buy organic, then at least purchase a natural produce spray that can remove the topical pesticides and chemicals.

Whole Foods
Eat whole foods, as free of processing as possible. Stay away from anything "white" if it is not a vegetable or fruit. This includes white, processed flours and sugars. Eat

whole grains instead of refined grains. Also, don't eat anything you cannot pronounce, or if you do not know what it is (this will free you of all the chemical additives and preservatives).

Coffee
If you are trying to get off the coffee habit, do it in stages to avoid the caffeine withdrawal headaches. I suggest that if you are drinking regular coffee, grind your own (organic) beans and use 1/2 regular and 1/2 decaffeinated coffee. The next week, use 3/4 decaffeinated and 1/4 regular coffee. The next week, switch to only decaffeinated. Then try using decaffeinated green teas or ginseng teas. These can provide a lift without the caffeine. Yerba Matte is also another coffee alternative.

Sugar
Try using more natural forms of sweetener. Stay away from the chemical sugar replacements. Corn syrups, cane juice and other types of sweeteners should also be avoided. Using maple syrup and honey are better than using refined sugars. Try Stevia (a natural herbal sweetener that does not affect blood sugar). Try sweetening with fruit or fruit juices. I like a little apple juice in my soups for sweetening. If you have a sugar tooth, go for the fruits, rather than pastries and candies. One of my favorite sweet substitutes are dates rolled in chopped almonds or pecans.

Raw/Live Foods
Another way to transition to a healthier diet is to eat some raw produce at every meal. This could be a salad, vegetable strips, fruit salad, etc. By eating something raw at every meal, you are providing your body with many electrolytes, enzymes and nutrients. Try a sandwich piled high with sprouts, shredded carrots and other vegetables. Use avocado or humus rather than mayonnaise.

Introduction

Super Green Foods
Adding in at least one serving a day of Super Green foods (see the "Nutrient Dense Super Foods" section) can help provide your body with many whole food nutrients and energy. This can also help decrease food cravings for "junk foods." Super Green foods can also help curb the appetite.

Fiber
Adding a serving of psyllium husk powder or ground flax seed (mixed in water on an empty stomach) can also help keep your bowel movements regular, keep the intestines cleaned out and help curb cravings. It is also used for weight loss.

80 / 20 Guideline
Try to eat 80% alkaline-forming foods in your diet and only 20% acid-forming foods. This will help balance your pH levels and replenish your electrolytes. See "pH Information."

Water
Drink purified or spring water instead of tap water. Tap water has chlorine and other chemicals that are not good for your health. Spring water has the added benefit of minerals. Distilled water is good during cleanse programs to help remove toxins from the body.

Smoking
If you are smoking and can't seem to quit, then try lobelia (herb) tea. Lobelia has lobeline, which can fill the same receptor sites as nicotine, but is not habit forming. There may be an herbal "smoking remedy" in your health food store. If you can't get away from the smoking ritual, then try smoking lobelia herb mixed with colt's foot herb. These two herbs can make a nice smoking substitute and the colt's foot soothes the lung tissue. If you absolutely cannot

give up the cigarettes yet, then at least switch to a chemical-free and additive-free cigarette, like "American Spirit," which is 100% tobacco and free of the added toxins. (Call 1-800-332-5595 for a list of stores).

Exercise
Adding at least 20 to 30 minutes of cardiovascular exercise 3 or 4 times a week can greatly improve health, attitude, disposition and metabolism. Adding two weight-resistance sessions a week can increase metabolism and prevent bone mass loss.

Introduction

What to Eat During and After Cleansing?

During the cleansing process, it is necessary to eat foods that encourage the detoxification and healing process. The tendency in most people's diets is to eat too many acid-forming foods. This creates imbalance problems in the body. The recipes in this cookbook include fresh and wholesome foods with a more alkaline pH level. This promotes healing and cleansing of the entire internal system and assists in balancing the body's pH level.

The following is a list of foods to avoid while cleansing: all canned, frozen, and processed foods; fried foods, sugar, salt, white flour products, dairy, meats, alcohol, caffeine, soy products, vinegar (except apple cider vinegar), seeds and nuts (unless sprouted), and oils (except flax seed and extra virgin olive oil).

Eat fresh organic produce when possible. Whole grains like quinoa, millet, and amaranth may be eaten. Fresh vegetable and fruit juices, herbal teas, extra virgin olive oil and flax seed oil and sprouted seeds are also good to use. Consult your individual cleanse program for additional recommendations.

After the cleanse and detoxification process, I recommend a diet that promotes a healthy acid-alkaline balance in the body (at least 80% alkaline foods), with as many pure, fresh, natural foods as possible. Eliminate chemically treated and processed foods from the diet.

Following are lists of recommended foods to eat while cleansing and foods to avoid while cleansing.

Cleanse Food List (Acid vs. Alkaline)

Acid-producing (Do not consume during cleansing)

Alcohol
Beans, dried
Black pepper
Bread and crackers
Cake and pastries
Canned, frozen, or processed foods
Cereal (processed)
Chocolate
Coffee
Corn starch
Cranberries
Dairy (milk, cheese, eggs)
Distilled vinegar
Fish or shellfish
Fruits (glazed or sulfured)
Grains (except millet, quinoa, and amaranth)
Honey or molasses
Legumes (unless sprouted)
Mayonnaise or other processed condiments
Meat, fish or fowl
Nuts (except soaked almonds)
Oils (except flax seed or extra virgin olive oil)
Pasta
Plums
Popcorn
Prunes
Salt
Seeds (unless sprouted)
Soft drinks
Soy and tofu products
Sugar, saccharin, aspartame
Tea (except herbal)
Tobacco
Water (tap or carbonated)
Wheat products

Introduction

OK Foods (Alkaline-producing):

Almonds-soaked
Apple cider vinegar
Beans, fresh
Dried fruit, non-sulfured (dates, figs, raisins, etc.)
Fruit, fresh (except cranberries)
Fruit juice, fresh squeezed
Green foods (algae, spirulina, chlorella, barley grass, etc.)
Herbal teas
Herbs (fresh or dried)
Garlic
Maple syrup
Millet, quinoa, and amaranth
Oil (flax seed or extra virgin olive oil)
Potatoes and yams (in moderation during cleansing)
Vegetables, fresh (raw or cooked)
Vegetable juice, fresh squeezed
Vegetable soup or broth
Seeds (flax, pumpkin, squash, sunflower soaked in water)
Seasonings (natural, salt-free, chemical-free)
Sea vegetables (dulse, kelp, seaweed, etc.)
Sprouts (all types)
Stevia (natural herbal sweetener)
Water (purified, non-carbonated mineral, or distilled)
Wheat grass juice
Whey (goat only not cow)

Note: There are other foods considered to be alkaline by several sources. They have not been included in the above list because they are mucus forming, create congestion in the body, and interfere with the cleanse and detoxification process. It is highly recommended that these foods be avoided during the cleanse and detoxification process.

Cottage cheese, fat-free
Chicken breast, lean, chemical-free
Eggs, free-range only
Milk, raw organic (unpasturized)
Soy products - tofu and tempeh (fermented)
Yogurt, organic

Nutrient Dense Super Foods

The following is a brief summary of the most popular super foods and their benefits. I have focused on the super foods that are high in protein and are highly recommended during and after cleansing. There are many other super foods that I have not included.

Nutrient-dense super foods can have a profound therapeutic effect on health and are recommended during and after cleansing. One of the advantages of using super foods is that you can get the benefit of multiple servings of vegetables in a single serving. I recommend at least five servings of vegetables a day.

Super Green Foods: Algae

Algae are one of nature's most primitive foods---they're millions of years old. The most common types include spirulina, chlorella and blue green algae. I also call these algae the "Super Green Foods" (a group that also includes the wheat grasses and other cereal grasses). I take a wide-spectrum Super Green Food powder that includes spirulina, chlorella, blue green algae and other Super Green Foods. I prefer a powdered or capsule form because the high-heat process used to make most (not all) tablets can oxidize some of the nutrients. (Algae love to grow in murky water, so check to see where the algae were harvested to make sure the water source is not in a polluted area.) Caution: Super Green Foods (including the algae types) can be cleansing to the body, so I suggest starting in moderation and building slowly to ensure that cleansing reactions do not occur.

Super Green Foods are high in antioxidants, carotenoids, selenium, zinc and some vitamin C. Because they are whole foods, they are much more easily absorbed by the

Introduction

body (more bio-available) than isolated vitamins or supplements. Their protein is 95% assimilable, gram for gram, with all the essential amino acids in balance. Super Green Foods have a higher biological value (a measure that determines how well nutrients, especially protein, are absorbed in the body) than any other source of vegetable protein. They also contain more than 2,000 enzymes and are also very good for helping to balance pH levels in the body. The benefits of Super Green Foods seem to surpass even their nutrient composition---whether this is due to their bio-availability in the body, their high vibrational energy levels or some other unknown reason.

Spirulina and blue green algae can enhance the immune system by stimulating greater B-Cell production. (B-Cells are white blood cells in the bone marrow that are the parents of five classes of antibodies made in the body.) Spirulina and blue green algae boost the overall function of the immune system, help increase the production of macrophages that eat pathogens in the body, and help increase the production of "NK" cells (natural killer cells) that kill bad cells in the body (cytoxins), especially cancer cells. Chlorella helps increase T-4 cell production, which enhances immune system function and may even support the function of the thymus gland (which also produces T-Cells for the immune system).

Spirulina is a Super Green Food that is grown in both ocean and alkaline waters. It is a complete protein that is highly digestible and works well with the pancreas. It is a recommended Super Green Food for hypoglycemia and chronic fatigue. Spirulina specializes in giving the body more physical energy. Because it provides energy, some cleansers will experience a "racy feeling" when they take it by itself. This can be remedied by mixing it with other types of Super Green Foods.

Blue green algae is a phyto-plankton with high amounts of digestible protein and enzymes. It is rich in vitamin B-12 and other B-Complex vitamins and has an abundance of beta carotene, fiber, chlorophyll and chelated minerals. It also has the highest amount of vitamin E of the algae family. It is a good source of gamma linoleic acid (GLA), an essential fatty acid that has been shown to have a beneficial effect in the treatment of cardiovascular disease and PMS. Blue green algae specializes in giving more mental clarity and enhancing mental and nervous functions. Because it is the most potent of the algae family, dosages are much smaller. Blue green algae has a positive effect on the hypothalamus, pineal and pituitary glands. The only commercial source for blue green algae is Klamath Lake, which is very alkaline and contains volcanic ash (a mineral-rich soil).

Chlorella is the most alkaline of the algae family. Chlorella is a one-celled algae grown as a super food. Chlorella is a complete protein, high in amino acids, beta carotene, minerals and all of the B vitamins. It also contains one of the highest concentrations of chlorophyll in the plant kingdom (other than wheat grass). Chlorophyll is recommended for iron-deficient types of anemia. Chlorella has an extremely beneficial effect on the health of the bowel and can stimulate peristaltic activity, help detoxify the colon, and promote the growth of helpful bacteria. It can eliminate heavy metals from the body because it is high in fiber and high in cellulose. Cellulose binds to heavy metals in the body, including lead, cadmium and mercury, and then removes them from the body. When eaten on a regular basis, chlorella helps to strengthen liver function, provides an increase in sustained energy and has a positive effect on the immune system. Chlorella can also protect against atherosclerosis because it is high in essential fatty acids and can reduce LDL cholesterol levels.

Introduction

Super Green Foods: Cereal Grasses
Many Super Green Food products include the cereal grasses in their formulas. Cereal grasses include wheat grass, alfalfa, barley and kamut. They are best used in their non-pasteurized form. They can be taken as a fresh juice or in powdered or capsule form. Again, I recommend staying away from tablets unless you have checked the processing methods. It is best to use small amounts of the cereal grasses regularly, rather than large amounts less often.

Barley grass contains powerful antioxidants, including vitamins C and E, carotenoids, selenium and SOD (an antioxidant produced internally by the body). It is helpful in restoring the liver and is an excellent food for those with anemia.

Wheat grass contains 25% protein, is very bio-available for the body and has a balanced amino acid profile. People who are allergic to wheat can use wheat grass because it does not contain gluten. It is also a good source for the antioxidant S.O.D., helps pull lead and cadmium out of the body and helps pull toxins out of the lymph nodes. It is a powerhouse of vitamins, minerals and chlorophyll (containing up to 70% chlorophyll). It is an overall cleanser and rebuilder for the body.

Other Super Foods
Nutritional yeast are colonies of tiny, one-celled plants grown specifically for human consumption. Their taste is a good indication of their quality – the better their taste the better the quality. They are a great source of B-vitamins (all except B-12, though recently B-12 has been added). They are abundant in protein (50% protein) and have a good balance of essential amino acids. They tend to chelate, bond and reduce the levels of heavy metals in the body, including lead, mercury and uranium. They are also high in niacin, which detoxifies the body by releasing fat-

stored toxins. (Niacin is also good for mood imbalances and mental disorders). Nutritional yeast also offers protection against common pollutants and the side effects of prescription drugs. Nutritional yeast should not be confused with Brewer's Yeast or Baker's Yeast. Nutritional yeast taste better than Brewer's Yeast and can be used as a seasoning for foods or added to smoothies. Nutritional yeast does not aggravate candida yeast growth like Baker's Yeast does because it does not contain live yeast cells.

Bees gathering the male reproductive parts of flower pollen make bee pollen. Bee pollen contains 56 essential nutrients for humans. It is high in minerals, especially in calcium and magnesium. It contains 25% to 50% protein, 15% healthy fats (including lecithin and essential fatty acids) and is high in natural lithium (which is good for bi-polar disorders). Bee pollen is considered to be a high-energy food for the body and is rapidly absorbed and utilized by the body. It also strengthens immune system function, especially spleen function, and can help with allergies. For allergies, it is suggested to start with small amounts and build up gradually.

Introduction

Super Green Food Smoothie Recipe
by Christine Dreher

In a blender or VitaMix add:

2 cups purified water
**1 ripe banana (I like to freeze them) or 1 cup of your
	favorite fruit**
**2 Tbs. (you can gradually use up to 4 Tbs.) of your
	favorite Super Green Algae mix**
1 tsp. Bee Pollen
1 Tbs. of Flax Seed Oil
1 Tbs. of Nutritional Yeast
Fresh apple juice to taste (optional)

Blend until smooth and drink.

Sources of Protein While Cleansing

Many sources of protein have been described in the previous section "Nutrient Dense Super Foods." These would include the algae family: Spirulina, Blue Green Algae, and Chlorella, the cereal grasses (Wheat Grass, Barley Grass, etc.), Nutritional Yeast and Bee Pollen.

Also, soaked almonds can be a good source of protein while cleansing. Almonds contain about 20% protein. They are very high in linoleic acid (a good fat). They are also very high in Vitamin E, Calcium, and contain some B vitamins. Soaking the almonds removes the enzyme inhibitors from the nuts, making them more digestible to the body. These can be added to salads, vegetables, included in smoothies (see the Almond Milk recipe) or eaten by themselves as snacks. Be sure not to soak more than you can eat in a day or two and store in the refrigerator to prevent molding.

Millet, described in the grain section is a nonglutenous grain. It is the most alkaline of the grains and the least congesting. It contains about 15% protein and has high amounts of fiber, niacin, thiamin, and riboflavin, iron, magnesium, and potassium.

Quinoa is a South and Central American grain that is also high in protein, iron and calcium. It also includes many of the B-vitamins and other minerals.

Amaranth is a Central American grain and is high in protein, calcium, iron and contains most of the B vitamins. Like millet and quinoa it is also a good source of dietary fiber.

Introduction

Sprouts (including aduki, alfalfa, buckwheat, clover, fenugreek, garbanzo, lentil, mung, radish, soybean and sunflower) are also great for cleansing and have 15 to 30% more protein than in it's unsprouted seeds due to the conversion of carbohydrates from seeds. Sprouts are also high in enzymes and many other vitamins and minerals.

Legumes and beans also have high levels of protein, but are discouraged (or greatly limited) during cleansing unless sprouted. Vegetables also contain some protein depending on the variety.

After cleansing, more varieties of protein can be reintroduced to the diet. In order to keep the pH balanced, I recommend eating about 80% alkaline forming foods and only 20% acid forming foods after cleansing.

Juicing

Juicing is a great way to receive an abundance of nutrients quickly and is great for cleansing and pH balance. Juicing allows cleansers to get the nutritional benefits of many more fruits or vegetables than would be possible by eating them whole. Because of the high levels of naturally occurring sugars in the sweeter juices, I recommend diluting sweeter juices by 50% water. For people with blood sugar problems, juicing may have to be modified to balance blood sugar levels. Juices have the pulp and fibers removed. Fiber helps to slow down the assimilation of glucose (sugar) into the blood stream, which prevents peaks and drops of blood sugar levels. For sugar sensitive cleansers, you may want to blend the whole fruit or vegetable in a blender (my favorite is a Vita Mix) with some purified water to retain the fiber and pulp. Or this can be accomplished with a juicer, by adding back in some of the pulp that is extracted by juicing.

The following are some great juice suggestions by Phyllis Avery, from her book *The Garden of Eden Raw Fruit and Vegetable Recipes*. Phyllis is also the creator of the raw, dehydrated vegetable seasonings. See "Seasonings" in the Resource Section for more information.

"Use only fresh, ripe vegetables, preferably organically grown. If regular supermarket quality produce is used, they should be washed carefully. Make only the amount of juice that will be used immediately. In storage, even under refrigeration, raw juices oxidize rapidly and lose their nutrients after 20 minutes. Sweet juices such as carrot, beet, grape, apple or pear juice should be diluted with 50% water or mixed with other less sweet juices.

Introduction

Never mix fruit and vegetable juices together. The combining of these two classes of foods can impair digestion assimilation, resulting in gas with only partial assimilation of nutrients. Drink vegetable or fruit juices between meals or one hour before meals but never with meals. Drink juices slowly and salivate well.

Suggestions - Combine the following groups in a juicer:

- 2 or 3 Tomatoes, 1 Celery Stalk, 1 Beet, 1 small Cucumber.

- 2 or 3 Tomatoes, 1 Celery Stalk, 1 Beet, 1 small Cucumber, 1 cup Cabbage.

- Any green tops (Parsley, Spinach, Kale, Swiss Chard, Turnip Tops, or Radish Tops) mixed with Carrot, Tomato, String Beans

- Avocado, Lettuce, Carrots, String Beans, Bell Peppers.

- 2 or 3 Tomatoes, 1 Celery Stalk, 2 inch bottom length of Daikon.

- 3 or 4 Carrots, 1 small Jicama, a small Tomatillo (Mexican Tomato), 1/2 cup Parsley.

- 1 large Cucumber, 1 large Beet, 1 cup Sprouts, handful String Beans.

- 2 or 3 Tomatoes, 1/2 cup Corn, 1 or 2 Parsnips, fresh Basil

- Tomato, Celery, Green Pepper, Cucumber, one Tbs. Lemon Juice (or can use 1 Tbs. soy when not cleansing), 1 tsp. Celery Seed.

- Tomatoes, Tomatillos, Yellow Bell Pepper, Lemon Juice, Dulse

- 1/4 cup of sprouted Sunflower Seeds can be added to each group for a creamy drink."

Seasoning and Flavoring Foods

The best and most natural seasonings to use in cleanse cooking are fresh herbs. Some of my favorites are: dill, basil, oregano, chives, cilantro, and garlic. I also enjoy cooking with Indian spices, including turmeric, cumin, and curry powder. Dried herbs work too if you do not have access to fresh herbs. If using dried herbs in recipes that call for fresh herbs, use 1/3 of the amount.

While cleansing, it is very important to stay away from salt (including sea salt) and black pepper. And I recommend using dulse (dried seaweed) instead of salt and cayenne pepper instead of black pepper. Fresh lemon juice adds a lot of flavor to food also. Apple cider vinegar is the only vinegar that should be used while cleansing and it adds a lot of flavor to foods. Nutritional yeast is also tasty in salads, soups and casserole dishes and is high in vegetable protein.

Be careful using prepared seasoning mixes because they often contain salt, sugar, monosodium glutamate, soy, or other ingredients that will interfere with the cleanse process. Also stay away from soy-based products while cleansing. Other spice blends are available in your local health food store.

I like using "Bernard Jensen's Vegetable Seasoning" as a vegetable broth base or as a seasoning in all types of grains, soups and vegetable dishes. It is available in most health food stores. Another wonderful vegetable seasoning is the raw, dehydrated vegetable seasonings "Tomato Tornado," "Veggie Valley," "Popcorn Pizzazz," and "Potato Picnic," by Phyllis Avery. See "Seasonings" in the Resources and References section in the back of the book for ordering information regarding these products.

Introduction

Throughout the cookbook, I mention a cooking method called dry sauté. This method of cooking uses no oils. Instead, the food is cooked in a non-stick skillet. The foods cook in their own natural juices. The key to dry sautéing is to use a utensil to frequently turn the food while cooking. This helps maintain the juiciness and flavor of the food. A little lemon juice, vegetable broth, tomato juice (from low acid tomatoes), or water can be added to the pan to prevent sticking and burning.

Regarding oils, use only extra virgin olive oil and flax seed oil while cleansing. Flax seed oil should be refrigerated. Neither should be used to sauté or cook foods while cleansing because this causes the pH of the food to become more acidic. A little oil can be added to the food after cooking for flavor.

Olive oil has three grades. It is best to use the lowest acidity grade, which is extra virgin olive oil. This grade also has the fullest flavor. Virgin olive oil has a higher acidity level and a lighter flavor. Pure olive oil has the highest acidity level and the lightest flavor.

Extra-virgin olive oil from the first cold press means that the olives were pressed at a low temperature. In order to be considered extra-virgin, the oil must be between 0 and 1 percent acidity. Extra virgin olive oil is made from olives that are pressed immediately after picking (usually between 24 to 48 hours). It should be stored in a cool, dark area. Extra-virgin olive oil will stay fresh up to two years if kept away from heat and sunlight. Olive oil should not be refrigerated or frozen, as it can solidify at these temperatures. It can help increase the HDL levels (good cholesterol) and help decrease LDL levels (bad cholesterol).

Flax seed oil is high in essential fatty acids (the good fats). Essential fatty acids are vital to our health and well being. One of it's benefits is assisting in weight loss by adjusting the metabolism, which can increase the body's ability to burn excess calories. Flax seed oil should be kept refrigerated, away from direct light and air. It should only be used raw, never heated or cooked. I also like "Udo's Choice" which is a certified organic blend of nutritionally superior oils. It is available in the refrigerated section of most health food stores.

Flax seeds can also be ground in a coffee grinder and added to salads, vegetables or as a topping on fruit salads. This is a great way to get the nutritional benefits of flax, increase fiber and add a nice, nutty taste.

There are many suggestions for alternative seasonings throughout this cookbook. Experiment with different herbs and natural seasonings and give your taste buds a chance to experience new flavors.

Introduction

Stevia as a Sweetener

The following is a summary of information I compiled from literature made available by Wisdom of the Ancients, a manufacturer and distributor of Stevia. The following disclaimer is quoted from their product information brochure: "This brief review of the stevia plant and its world-wide uses in no way constitutes an endorsement of such uses. At this time the FDA permits stevia to be imported, labeled and sold only for its approved use as a dietary supplement and in skin care...This product is not intended to diagnose, treat, cure, or prevent any disease."

Stevia (stevia rebaudiana) is a natural herb from the rain forests of Paraguay. It possesses many medicinal healing properties, contains many nutrients (calcium, potassium, sodium, magnesium, zinc, rutin, iron, phosphorus, vitamins A and C, and more), and is used as a natural sweetener. It is one of the few sweeteners, with a true alkaline pH level. The purest form of stevia is the whole leaf plant, ground into either a fine powder or extracted into a concentrated water-based extract. I recommend staying away from the alcohol-based extracts or stevioside products. Stevioside products have the sweetening qualities of stevia, but do not have the nutritional benefits of pure stevia leaves.

Stevia has no calories and is much sweeter than sugar. It can be used in place of sugar in a variety of ways. An infusion can be made with 1 teaspoon of stevia leaves to 1 cup of water. One drop of the infusion equals about one half teaspoon of sugar. The ground stevia powder can be used in cooking or sprinkled on foods after cooking. There are also tea bags available containing the ground stevia powder. In the recipes contained in this cookbook, I suggest substituting stevia for honey or maple syrup. Be sure to add the stevia gradually, since it is sweeter than other sweeteners.

Introduction

When purchasing stevia, make sure it is of good quality. I understand that the highest quality comes from Paraguay. The brand I recommend is manufactured by a company called Wisdom of the Ancients. They have tea bags, liquid concentrate, and extract tablets. Check your local health food store or see the Resources and References section.

The nutritional benefits reported are amazing. Studies have shown that it has been used for years in South America to help regulate blood sugar for hypoglycemic and diabetic patients. Within a short time period, these studies indicated that people's blood glucose levels were normalized by adding 20 to 30 drops at each meal. It is also used as a weight loss aid because it contains no calories and seems to satisfy the "sweet tooth." Studies also indicate it can lower high blood pressure without affecting normal blood pressure. The tea is also used as a stomach and digestion tonic. It is also known to reduce the craving for tobacco and alcohol. The water-based liquid extract is also used on the skin to smooth out wrinkles and heal blemishes.

Approximate Stevia Sweetness Equivalents:

1/3 to 1/2 tsp. White Extract Powder = 1 cup sugar
1 tsp. Stevia Clear Liquid = 1 cup sugar
1 Tbs. Whole Leaf Dark Liquid Concentrate = 1 cup sugar
1-1/2 to 2 Tbs. Whole Leaf Dried Powder = 1 cup sugar
2 tsp. Whole Leaf Dark Liquid Concentrate = 1 cup sugar

Note: Too much Stevia may taste bitter. When substituting Stevia for sugar, you may have to adjust for the bulk. Try adding applesauce, mashed bananas, or apple juice.

Introduction

Organic Vs. Commercial Produce

What is organically grown food? It is food grown without the use of synthetic fertilizers, pesticides, fungicides or herbicides and processed without irradiation, which is a process of extending shelf life through the use of the nuclear power industry's by-products.

Organic farming is a philosophy that uses processes that nurture rather than deplete the soil in which the crops grow. Organic farmers use nature's own solutions to overcome problems, thereby reducing chemical contamination of the environment and contributing to the health of the land and the population now and for future generations.

One example of this type of farming is when farmers use cover crops, which are temporary crops used to contribute valuable nutrients when plowed under. They are able to maintain soil fertility by rotating crops and by adding natural nutrients, such as bone meal, fish meal, seaweed, or animal manure. They weed by hand rather than applying herbicides. And they encourage nature to participate in pest control by releasing predator insects instead of spraying with pesticides.

Organically grown produce is usually superior to commercial produce in nutritional value (depending on the mineral content of the soil) and superior in taste. Ingesting the toxic pesticide residues from commercial produce can increase health risks. Especially for children, whose physiologies are more susceptible to the effects of toxic pesticides.

What is pesticide-free or unsprayed produce? Produce that may have been grown with chemical fertilizers, but on which no pesticides are used beyond the bloom stage (therefore the fruit is unsprayed). Often growers will provide lab test results verifying that no chemical residues are present on the product. This description can also be used for produce that growers claim is organically grown but lacks the proper certification.

What is transitional organic produce? This is produce from a farm that is on its way to certification. When a farm converts from conventional growing practices to organic techniques, there is a one to three year wait, depending on the state laws, before becoming certified.

Conventional or commercial produce is grown with synthetic fertilizers, pesticides, and fungicides to aid, protect, and speed up the growth of the crops. Other chemicals are used to reduce labor costs and spoilage. There are natural produce sprays available in the health food stores that can remove topical waxes, chemicals, and pesticides.

In closing, some people do not buy organic because it can be more expensive, unless they can grow it themselves. The higher prices reflect the more labor intensive organic growing practices, such as weeding by hand instead of spraying herbicides, or the lengthy and expensive certification process.

Choosing to buy organic is supporting a natural system of agriculture that sustains and nourishes the soil and decreases the toxic pollution of the planet and contributes to one's health and well-being. For more information about organic foods, see the Resources and References section in the back of this book.

Introduction

The Cleanse Cookbook

Soups

Soups

Avocado Corn Soup (Raw)
by Jessie Ann, Chino Valley, AZ

2 ears raw corn
2 scallions
1/2 cup cabbage sprouts
1 bell pepper
1 small cucumber
1/2 avocado
Natural seasonings to taste (see "Seasoning and
    Flavoring Foods" in the Introduction)

See "About Corn" in the Vegetables section for more information.

Dice the vegetables and cut the corn from the cob. Blend in a blender until creamy. Put the avocado in the blender last. Serve at room temperature. Serves 1 to 2.

Beet Borsht Soup
by Sharna Gross, San Diego, CA

8 cups of vegetable stock (see recipe in this section)
6 large beets, cut in half and peeled
6 new potatoes, peeled and boiled whole

See "About Beets" and "About Potatoes" in the Vegetables section for more information.

Simmer the beets in the vegetable stock until the beets are soft. Remove the beets from the broth. Use one of the following two options:

Option 1: Slice the beets and potatoes and place them back in the broth. Serve hot.

Option 2: Puree 1/2 of the beets in a blender and put them back into the broth. Cool and slice the rest of the beets and potatoes and place them in the vegetable broth. Serve hot.

Makes 8 cups of soup.

Note: If the broth is not sweet enough, you may want to add some fresh apple juice or a little stevia.

Black Bean Soup
with Cilantro and Kale
by Sharna Gross, San Diego, CA

4 cups black beans, soaked, sprouted, and cooked
1 Tbs. cayenne pepper
1 bunch cilantro, finely chopped
1 Tbs. lime juice
1 bunch kale, finely chopped
1 Tbs. extra virgin olive oil or flax seed oil
4 cups vegetable stock (see recipe in this section)
1 onion, peeled and chopped
1 tsp. cumin seeds

In a non-stick pan, toast the cumin seeds until they become aromatic. Then cool and grind the seeds in a blender or coffee grinder. Set aside.

Dry sauté the onion with the finely chopped kale, adding a little stock if needed to maintain moisture. Cook until soft, then set aside.

Puree the beans with the stock and 2 Tbs. of cilantro, cumin, cayenne and lime juice in a blender. Place the pureed ingredients in a large pot, adding the onion and kale. Heat and serve, garnished with cilantro and oil. Makes 10 cups of soup.

Carrot Ginger Soup
by Sharna Gross, San Diego, CA

1 cup carrot juice, freshly squeezed
6 large carrots
5 cups of vegetable stock (see recipe in this section)
1 large onion, peeled and chopped
1 tsp. nutmeg
4 Tbs. ginger, chopped
1 Tbs. curry powder (optional)
1 tsp. parsley, chopped
1 ginger root

See "About Carrots" in the Vegetables section for more information.

Grate the ginger root and squeeze through a cheese cloth to yield 4 Tbs. of ginger juice. Boil all the ingredients, except the carrot and ginger juice, in a large soup pan or stock pot until the carrots are tender. Add the carrot and ginger juice and puree the ingredients in a blender. Serve hot.

Note: Curry powder is optional and can be added during the puree.

Gazpacho Soup (Raw)
by Sharon Skylor, San Francisco, CA

Soup:

1 onion, peeled and quartered
1 green pepper, peeled and quartered
1 cucumber, peeled, seeds removed, cut in chunks
2 cups fresh tomato juice from low-acid tomatoes
1 Tbs. apple cider vinegar
Dash of cayenne, to taste
Lemon juice, fresh squeezed, to taste

Garnish (all ingredients coarsely chopped):

1/2 cucumber
1 tomato, (vine-ripened or low-acid variety)
1/2 onion, peeled and quartered
1/2 green pepper
1 stalk celery
1 Tbs. extra virgin olive oil or flax seed oil
1 clove garlic, peeled and crushed
Dulse or other vegetable seasoning to taste (see
        "Seasoning and Flavoring Foods" in the
        Introduction)

Place all the soup ingredients in the food processor and
blend until smooth. Pour the soup in a container and
refrigerate for at least 2 hours until chilled. Note: if you
pre-chill the vegetables and tomato juice, you will not
need to wait for the soup to chill.

Stir in the garnish ingredients and seasonings. Serve
chilled. Serves 6.

Golden Squash Soup
by Peter Dyke, San Diego, CA

4 carrots
2 small garnet yams
4 celery stalks
2 Tbs. ginger, chopped
1 medium acorn squash
2 tsp. oregano, dried
1 tsp. lemon juice, freshly squeezed

Bring 8 cups of water to a boil. While waiting, cut the vegetables into bite-size pieces.

Dry sauté the vegetables in a large pot until aromatic (add a couple of drops of lemon juice for moisture). Then add enough of the boiling water to cover the top of the vegetables. Boil for 10 minutes. Add the oregano, then add the rest of the boiled water. Cover and simmer for 30 to 40 minutes.

Ladle the contents of the pan into the blender and blend until smooth. Serves 4 to 6.

Note: For a touch of sweetness, add a touch of stevia, honey, or maple syrup.

Jerusalem Artichokes and Onion Soup
by Emily Mudhur Fung

4 Shiitake mushrooms
1 large onion, peeled and chopped
1 tsp. thyme, dried
5 or 6 medium Jerusalem artichokes, peeled and
        chopped

See "About Jerusalem Artichokes" in the Vegetables
section for more information.

Soak the mushrooms for 20 minutes in hot water. Drain
the mushrooms, then boil with the rest of the ingredients
in a pint of water until tender. Serve hot. Serves 2.

Mushroom Millet Soup
by Sharna Gross, San Diego, CA

1 lb. shiitake mushrooms, sliced
1 celery stalk, diced
1 lb. domestic mushrooms, sliced
1 yellow onion, peeled and diced
1 lb. Portobello mushrooms, sliced
1 1/2 cups millet, cooked (see Grains section)
Fresh thyme, handful, diced
3/4 gallon vegetable stock (see recipe in this section)

See "About Mushrooms" in the Vegetables section for more information.

Dry sauté the onion, celery, and thyme in a large non-stick skillet (adding a teaspoon of vegetable stock for moisture), until the onions are soft and golden-colored. Set aside in a bowl.

Dry sauté the mushrooms in batches so they are also golden and soft. Combine the mushrooms with the onions, celery and herbs.

Then, in a blender, puree 1/2 of the vegetable stock, half of the sautéed vegetable mixture, and one cup of the millet. The mixture will be very thick. Transfer to a soup pot and add the remaining vegetable stock, sautéed vegetable mix, and millet. Heat and serve. Makes one gallon of soup.

Pesto Vegetable Soup
by Ivi Turner, San Diego, CA

3 quarts distilled water
1/2 cup fava beans, soaked, sprouted, and cooked
1 onion, peeled and chopped
2 carrots, diced
1/2 green cabbage, chopped small
2 leeks, chopped (white part only)
2 celery stalks, chopped
1 turnip, diced
2 potatoes, diced
2 tomatoes (vine-ripened, low-acid), seeded, diced
1/2 cup snap peas, shelled
1/2 cup green beans, diced
1 zucchini, diced
4 garlic cloves, peeled
10 basil leaves
1 Tbs. extra virgin olive oil or flax seed oil

Boil the water. Add the beans, onions, carrots, cabbage, leeks, celery, turnips, and potatoes. Simmer for 45 minutes or until the beans are tender. Add the tomatoes, snap peas, green beans, and zucchini. Simmer for 10 minutes.

In the meantime, make the pesto sauce by crushing the garlic with the basil leaves in a food processor or blender until they make a paste. Add the oil a little at a time. Add the pesto sauce to your soup just before serving. Serves 8.

Potato Leek Soup
by Sharna Gross, San Diego, CA

1/2 gallon of vegetable stock (see recipe in this section)
1/4 cup Italian parsley, chopped
2 large leeks, chopped
2 sprigs fresh tarragon, chopped
4 large potatoes, peeled
1 large onion, peeled and chopped
2 cloves garlic, peeled and minced
2 tsp. vegetable seasoning (see "Seasoning and
    Flavoring Foods" in the Introduction)

See "About Potatoes" in the Vegetables section for more information.

Dry sauté the leeks, onion, and garlic until soft. Boil the potatoes until soft. Puree all the ingredients together, including the vegetable stock, in a blender. Heat the pureed mixture, over medium heat, for a few minutes to desired temperature. Makes 3/4 of a gallon of soup.

Note: Christine recommends adding fresh lemon juice to taste, for a zesty flavor.

Raw Soup
by Jamey Dina, N.D. and Kim Sproul, N.D., Escondido, CA
From their cookbook *Uncooking with Jamey & Kim*

Add the following ingredients to taste:

Carrot Juice Dressing (see Dressing section)
Cucumber or celery
Fresh corn, cut off cob
Soft summer squash (zucchini, crookneck, sunburst)
Purple onion, broccoli, or any other vegetable you like
**Herbs: arugula, cilantro, basil, tarragon, thyme, or
     rosemary**
Spices: cumin, curry, turmeric (optional)
**Any other desired seasonings (optional; see "Seasoning
     and Flavoring Foods" in the Introduction)**

In a blender, blend the cucumber or celery into the carrot
juice dressing. Add any of the optional herbs, spices, or
seasonings and blend in. This is your broth.

Then shred the squash and other vegetables lengthwise
and stir them, along with the corn, into the broth.

Experiment with different ingredients for a different soup,
or slightly warm it on the stove. Keep the temperature as
low as possible and put a thermometer in the soup. Make
sure the temperature does not go above 100°F. This way,
you can have warm, raw soup!

Roasted Garlic and Fennel Soup
by Sharna Gross, San Diego, CA

1 Tbs. vegetable seasoning (see "Seasoning and
    Flavoring Foods" in the Introduction)
2 large carrots
3 Tbs. extra virgin olive oil or flax seed oil
6 heads of garlic
2 stalks of celery, coarsely chopped
2 heads of fennel, coarsely chopped
1 large onion, peeled and coarsely chopped
1 cup fresh apple juice
4 cups vegetable stock (see recipe in this section)
2 Tbs. Italian parsley, chopped

Preheat oven to 400°.

Place all the vegetables, apple juice and garlic in a large
baking pan, cover with foil, and roast in the oven until the
garlic heads are soft and the garlic can be easily pressed
out.

Press the garlic out of the heads into the blender. Be sure
to discard the skins. Add all the other ingredients into the
blender and puree. Serve hot with a parsley garnish.
Makes 8 cups of soup.

Roasted Sweet Pepper and Tomato Soup
by Ivi Turner, San Diego, CA

3 red bell peppers
1 fresh ancho (pasilla) chile
10 Roma tomatoes (vine-ripened, low-acid)
1/2 cucumber
1 cup garlic cloves, whole and peeled
1/2 cup extra virgin olive oil flax seed oil
1/4 cup apple cider vinegar
6 oz. fresh vegetable juice, tomato-based (optional)

Roast the bell peppers and Ancho peppers under a broiler until the skin blackens. Put the peppers in a small bowl and cover. Peel the tomatoes by dropping them in boiling water for 20 seconds. Remove them and quickly plunge them into cold water. Cut in half and gently press out the seeds.

Peel the cucumber, cut it in half, and strip out the seeds with the back of a teaspoon. Poach the garlic cloves in the oil slowly, using low heat, until they are soft and white. By now the peppers should be cooled, so peel them under water and strip out the seeds. Put everything in a blender and blend well. Chill thoroughly.

Note: Depending on the size and moisture content of the vegetables, the consistency may vary. You may want to have a 6 oz. bottle of fresh vegetable juice (tomato-based) to keep the blender flowing smoothly. Serves 2.

Spinach Fennel Soup
by Sharna Gross, San Diego, CA

1 head of fennel, sliced
1 large onion, peeled and sliced
2 large carrots, chopped
3 bunches of spinach
6 cups vegetable stock (see recipe in this section)
2 Tbs. lemon juice, freshly squeezed
1 tsp. apple cider vinegar

Preheat oven to 400°.

Place the fennel, onion, and carrots in a roasting pan and roast them in the oven until the onion and fennel are soft and golden-colored. In a blender, puree the roasted vegetables with the rest of the ingredients. Serve hot. Makes 8 cups.

Spinach, New Potato, and Almond Soup
Estelle Russom, New Kirk, OK

1 to 2 cups cooked chopped spinach
6 to 8 cooked new potatoes, with skin, boiled
1 medium-large onion, dry sautéed
12 to 16 soaked almonds (soak overnight)
Seasoning to taste

Puree the almonds in a blender or food processor until chopped fine. Add the other ingredients and puree, except hold 1 or 2 of the potatoes aside.

Heat in a saucepan if using leftovers from the refrigerator. You will need to use a splash of water, vegetable broth or the potato water to thin the soup (if not cleansing, you could use rice or soy milk).

Add the reserved potatoes, and break apart with a fork. This will add to the texture of the soup. Garnish with sliced green onion, dill weed, parsley or green of your choice.

Tomato Basil Soup
by Sharna Gross, San Diego, CA

1 cup vegetable stock (see recipe in this section)
2 cloves garlic, peeled and chopped
20 roma tomatoes (or vine-ripened, low-acid tomatoes)
1 large onion, peeled and chopped
1 bunch of basil

Preheat oven to 400°.

Place the onion, garlic, and tomatoes in a roasting pan and roast them in the oven until tender. If browning occurs before the tomatoes are soft, cover them with foil and continue roasting.

Cook the vegetable stock in a small saucepan, over medium heat, until it comes to a boil. Set aside.

Remove the roasted ingredients from the oven and soft puree them in a blender with the basil and the heated vegetable stock. Serve hot. Makes 1/2 gallon of soup.

Vegetable Stock or Clear Vegetable Soup with Millet

by Sharna Gross, San Diego, CA

Chop the following ingredients coarsely for the vegetable stock:

1 cup celery	1/2 cup zucchini squash
1 cup carrot	1 cup asparagus
1 onion, peeled	1 cup beet greens
3 cloves garlic, peeled	1/2 cup cauliflower
1 cup broccoli (no crowns)	1 cup of whole mushrooms
1 or 2 bay leaves (optional)	

Place the ingredients in two gallons of purified water and simmer lightly for 3 to 4 hours until the liquid has been reduced by half. (Christine likes to add 2 dried bay leaves to the water.) Discard the cooked vegetables. This is the basic vegetable stock, which can be used as a base for many recipes. Makes 1 gallon of stock. You can freeze the extra broth in freezer bags for future use.

To make the clear vegetable soup, while the vegetable stock is simmering, dice the following vegetables into bite-size pieces:

1 cup carrots	1 cup broccoli crowns
1 cup zucchini	1 cup asparagus tips
1 cup mushrooms	1 cup celery
1 cup kale or spinach	2 cups cooked millet
Vegetable seasoning or dulse (optional; see "Seasoning and Flavoring Foods" in the Introduction)	

Add the diced vegetables and optional seasoning to the stock and simmer slowly until the vegetables are soft. (Christine likes to add 1 Tbs. or more of vegetable seasoning or dulse.) Don't overcook. Add 2 cups of cooked millet and serve hot.

Wild Mushroom Soup
with Onion Puree
by Sharna Gross, San Diego, CA

1 lb. domestic mushrooms, sliced
1 tsp. rosemary, dried
1 lb. shiitake mushrooms, sliced
6 to 8 cups vegetable stock (see recipe in this section)
1 lb. crimini mushrooms, sliced
1 large brown onion, peeled and chopped
2 cloves garlic, peeled and chopped

Note: You may want to start with the Onion Puree (see below) because it requires a preheated oven and roasting time.

Dry sauté the mushrooms and onions until golden brown. Add the garlic toward the end so the garlic does not brown. (You may need to sauté in batches, or use a large skillet.)

Puree 1/2 of the mushrooms and garlic in a blender with the stock and rosemary; chop the other 1/2 coarsely and combine it with the pureed ingredients in a soup pan. Serve hot. Makes 8 cups of soup.

Onion puree (garnish for soup):

3 red onions, peeled and chopped
1 Tbs. apple cider vinegar
1 Tbs. extra virgin olive oil or flax seed oil

Preheat oven to 400°.

Roast the onions in a roasting pan covered with foil until soft. Puree in a blender with the apple cider vinegar and oil. Garnish the soup with 1 Tbs. or more of the puree.

Salads

Salads

The Cleanse Cookbook

Beet Salad
by Ivi Turner, San Diego, CA

4 to 5 whole beets, greens removed
1 red onion, peeled and sliced
Apple cider vinegar, to taste
Dulse, to taste
5 carrots, julienne-sliced
Extra virgin olive oil or flax seed oil, to taste
Red pepper flakes, to taste

See "About Beets" in the Vegetables section for more information.

Steam the beets until tender; cool and remove the skins. Julienne (slice into strips) the beets into large pieces. Briefly steam the carrots until they are bright orange. Then cool the carrots in ice water.

Toss the beets, carrots, and sliced red onion. Add the oil and vinegar to taste. Toss to coat. Add the dulse and a pinch of red pepper flakes. Toss well, place in a covered container, and store in the refrigerator.

This salad will keep several days, and the vegetables will continue to marinate and become tart. Serves 4 to 5.

Option: Cut carrots diagonally and beets in slices.

Christine recommends using the beet greens in the "Vegetable Stock" recipe in the Soups section.

Beyond Salad
by Laura Sellens, Missoula, MT

1 bunch of spinach, cleaned
1 head of lettuce, cleaned and torn into pieces
1 handful of alfalfa sprouts
2 small carrots, sliced or grated
3- to 4-inch chunk daikon, sliced or grated
1 bunch of green onions, chopped
2 tomatoes (vine-ripened, low-acid), sliced
1/4 to 1/2 lb. Shiitake mushrooms, chopped
1 or 2 yellow, green or red peppers, chopped
1 bunch of parsley, chopped
1 handful of fresh basil, chopped
1 handful of sunflower sprouts
3 beets, grated
3- to 4-inch chunk of burdock root, grated
1/2 head of cabbage, shredded
1 or 2 avocados, cut in small slices
1 head of broccoli flowers, cut into bite-size pieces
Garlic, crushed and peeled, to taste

Toss all the ingredients except tomatoes and avocados, which should be sprinkled on top.

Note: The chunks of vegetables shift to the bottom, so mix well. Serves 4 to 6.

Option: Serve with garlic dressing (see the Dressings section).

Colorful Rainbow Salad
by Christine Dreher, San Diego, CA

1 carrot, shredded
1 cup purple cabbage, shredded
2 roma tomatoes (vine-ripened, low-acid)
1 small, ripe avocado or 1/2 large avocado
1 ear raw corn
1 or 2 celery stalks
1/2 cup of sprouted sunflower seeds
1/2 cup of jicama, diced

Cut the corn from the cob. Cut the tomatoes, avocado, celery, and jicama into bite-size pieces. Place all the ingredients into a salad bowl. Toss lightly.

Serve with either lemon oil, or sweet and sour dressing (see recipe in the Dressings section). Serves 1 to 2.

Corn Salad
with Steamed and Dressed Asparagus
by Ivi Turner, San Diego, CA

1/2 lb. asparagus
1/2 cup apple cider vinegar
1/4 cup extra virgin olive oil or flax seed oil
1 Tbs. mint, chopped
1 Tbs. basil, chopped
Dulse and cayenne, to taste
2 cups sweet corn, cut from cob
1 avocado, peeled and sliced
1 green onion, minced

See "About Asparagus" and "About Corn" in the
Vegetables section for more information.

Blanch the asparagus in hot water for 5 minutes or until
tender when pricked with a fork. Set aside to cool.

Combine 1/4 cup of the apple cider vinegar, oil, and
herbs. Season with dulse and cayenne. Mix in the corn,
avocado, and onion.

On a large platter, lay a strip of the corn salad at an angle
across from the asparagus diagonally. Alternate with
strips of corn salad and asparagus. Serves 4.

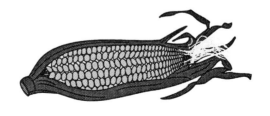

The Cleanse Cookbook

Jicama Garnish
by Ivi Turner, San Diego, CA

1 large jicama, cubed
2 cucumbers, cubed
2 medium red onions, peeled and cubed
3 tomatoes (vine-ripened, low-acid), cut into chunks
1/4 cup maple syrup (or stevia to taste)
Apple cider vinegar, to taste
Bottled or purified water

In a large glass mixing bowl, combine the jicama,
cucumbers, onions, and tomatoes. Add a little stevia or
maple syrup, to taste. Cover the vegetables with one part
vinegar and three parts water. Marinate for one hour
before serving. Serves 2 to 4.

Layered Salad
by Sharna Gross, San Diego, CA

3 large tomatoes (vine-ripened, low-acid), cut in 1/2 inch
      slices
1 large red onion, peeled and sliced thin
1 cup fresh basil leaves
1 avocado, sliced thin
Raw pesto (see recipe in Sauces and Dips section)
Citrus vinaigrette (see Dressings section)

In a shallow, porcelain dish, layer the tomato, onion, basil, and avocado in 3 layers and pour the citrus vinaigrette on top of the layers to marinate thoroughly. After an hour or so, serve the salad with a dollop of raw pesto. Serves 2 to 3.

Millet and Three Mushroom Salad with Baby Spinach
by Ivi Turner, San Diego, CA

2 cups distilled or purified water
1 cup millet, soaked
1/2 onion, peeled and chopped
4 cloves garlic, peeled and chopped
2 bay leaves
2 cups mushrooms, shiitake, crimini or white
1 bunch of parsley, finely chopped
1 bunch of green onions, finely chopped
1/4 cup apple cider vinegar
2 cups spinach, cleaned
Juice of 1 lemon
Roasted eggplant (garnish)

See "About Eggplant" in the Vegetables section for more information about eggplant and the Grains section for more information about millet.

Bring the water to a boil in a large pot. Add the millet, onion, garlic, and bay leaves; cover and simmer until cooked. Remove from heat and cool.

Coarsely chop the mushrooms and toss them into the cooked millet mixture. Add the parsley, green onion, and apple cider vinegar.

In a separate bowl, toss the spinach with the lemon juice. Place the spinach in the middle of a serving platter and ring the millet salad around the spinach. Garnish with the roasted eggplant. Serves 4 to 6.

New Potato and Asparagus Salad
Ivi Turner, San Diego, CA

3 Tbs. shallots, minced
6 medium red potatoes, cleaned
2 lbs. asparagus, cleaned
4 Tbs. chives, sliced
Dried mustard, to taste
2 Tbs. lemon juice
1/4 to 1/2 cup extra virgin olive oil or flax seed oil
Dulse or vegetable seasoning, to taste (see "Seasoning
       and Flavoring Foods" in the Introduction)
Cayenne pepper (optional)

See "About Potatoes" and "About Asparagus" in the
Vegetables section for more information.

Cook the potatoes in the water, with dulse or other
vegetable seasoning, until tender. Let cool.

Cook the asparagus until crisp-tender. Drain and cool in
ice water.

Cut the potatoes into wedges. Cut the asparagus into 1 1/2
inch pieces. Toss them with the potatoes.

In a small bowl, combine the mustard with a little water to
create a smooth texture. Add the lemon juice. Gradually
whisk in the oil. Pour over the vegetables to coat. Add the
chives and shallots, then season with dulse and cayenne
pepper.

Place in a container and store in the refrigerator. Serve at
room temperature or a little warmer if you prefer. Serves 3
to 6.

Roasted Eggplant Salad
by Ivi Turner, San Diego, CA

1 large eggplant, cubed
2 red peppers, cut in 1-inch pieces
5 to 10 cloves garlic, peeled
2 stalks celery, cut in 1-inch pieces
1 large onion, peeled and cut in wedges
Juice of 1 lemon
Dulse or vegetable seasoning, to taste (see "Seasoning
    and Flavoring Foods" in the Introduction)
Cayenne pepper, to taste
Extra virgin olive oil or flax seed oil, to taste

Preheat oven to 450°.

Place all the vegetables in a single layer in a non-stick
roasting pan. Squeeze the lemon juice over them. Sprinkle
with dulse, or other vegetable seasonings.

Bake, uncovered, for about 20 minutes, turning with a
spatula several times as they brown. Drizzle with oil and
add more seasonings to taste. Serve hot or cold. Serves 2.

Option: Use zucchini and red peppers.

Note: The trick to this recipe is to make sure your oven is
hot.

Simple Salad
by Jamey Dina, N.D. and Kim Sproul, N.D., Escondido, CA
From their cookbook <u>Un</u>cooking with Jamey & Kim

Add amounts of the following according to taste:

Greens or sprouts (we recommend buckwheat greens)
Tomatoes (vine-ripened, low-acid)
Chives or scallions (we prefer chives)
Flax seed oil or extra virgin olive oil

Chop the tomatoes and the chives or scallions. Mix all the ingredients together for a simple, delicious and nutritious salad. No need to add dressing; the juices of the tomatoes, combined with the oil, provides it. This salad is very light and will digest quickly and easily.

Christine suggests adding a little chopped basil and crushed garlic in this salad.

Chives

Slaw
by Ivi Turner, San Diego, CA

1/2 medium cabbage, shredded
1/2 small red cabbage, shredded
1/2 lb. of broccoli stalks, shredded
4 carrots, shredded
1 bunch of cilantro, chopped
Extra virgin olive oil or flax seed oil, to taste
Apple cider vinegar, to taste
Pinch of red pepper flakes
Dulse or vegetable seasoning, to taste (see "Seasoning
    and Flavoring Foods" in the Introduction)

Toss the shredded vegetables together. Add the cilantro.
Add the oil and apple cider vinegar to taste. Toss lightly,
then add the dulse and a tiny pinch of red pepper flakes.
Toss again. Chill in refrigerator. Serves 4.

South of the Border Salad
by Christine Dreher, San Diego, CA

5 to 6 large leaves of green or red leaf lettuce, cleaned
1 carrot
1 large ear of corn
1/2 cup of fresh cilantro, chopped
1/2 cup red bell pepper, chopped
1/2 cup of red or green onion, chopped
12 to 15 sweet cherry tomatoes (vine-ripened, low-acid)
1/2 to 3/4 cup of sprouts, alfalfa or clover

Rinse all the vegetables thoroughly. Dry the lettuce; tear into bite size pieces and place in a medium size serving bowl. Shred the carrot and add to the bowl. Cut the corn off the cob and distribute on top of salad. Add the onion and peppers. Toss the salad until all the ingredients are mixed.

Place the cherry tomatoes on top of the salad in a circle along the inside rim of the bowl. Place the sprouts on top of the salad inside the tomato ring and spoon the avocado on top of the sprouts. Serves 2 to 3.

See the Dressings section for dressing suggestions. Christine recommends "Salsa Fresca."

Spinach Salad
with Browned Garlic and Dates
Ivi Turner, San Diego, CA

4 cloves garlic, peeled and sliced thin, browned in
        lemon juice, in a non-stick pan
6 Tbs. extra virgin olive oil or flax seed oil
6 Tbs. apple cider vinegar
2 tsp. maple syrup (or stevia to taste)
2 tsp. dried basil
1 tsp. dried thyme
Dash of dulse
Dash of cayenne
1 medium red bell pepper, sliced thin
3/4 cup non-sulfured dates, chopped
4 cups fresh spinach, washed, dried

In a large serving bowl, combine the garlic, oil, vinegar, stevia or maple syrup, and herbs, mixing well. Add a dash of dulse and cayenne to taste; adjust flavors if necessary. Add the bell pepper and dates and toss. Let stand for 1 hour. When ready to serve, add the spinach leaves and toss thoroughly. Serves 4 to 6.

Salads

Vegetables

Vegetables

About Vegetables
by Christine Dreher, San Diego, CA

Selection:

The best and freshest vegetables of course are from your own garden or farm. The next best is selecting the freshest produce available from your local farmer's market or health food store. Stay away from produce that looks old, wilted, bruised or discolored. If purchasing non-organic produce, wash it thoroughly to remove topical waxes and pesticides. There are vegetable washes available in health food stores that can be sprayed on produce to remove chemicals. My favorite is a grapefruit seed extract spray that works well and is totally natural.

Preparation:

When cleaning vegetables, do not soak them because this removes valuable nutrients and enzymes. Eating vegetables raw, when possible, is the best way to get maximum nutritional value.

When cooking vegetables, use as little water as possible, and do not overcook, to prevent loss of nutrients and enzymes. Steaming is better than boiling vegetables. I use a metal vegetable steamer that fits inside a large cooking pot with a lid. Add just enough water to coat the bottom of the pan but not enough to touch the steamer basket or vegetables. Be sure to distribute the vegetables loosely in the steamer to allow the steam to circulate around the vegetables and cook them evenly. A bigger pan and vegetable steamer work better because they allow more cooking space. Do not overcook the vegetables. When cooked, be sure to remove the pan lid and drain the steaming water because the steam will continue to cook the vegetables.

Vegetables

Dry sautéing vegetables is much better than cooking in oil or frying. The latter changes the pH level to more acidic instead of alkaline. You can add some lemon juice, vegetable broth or tomato juice (from low-acid or vine ripened tomatoes) when dry sautéing to prevent the vegetables from sticking. Also use a non-stick cooking pan.

Baking or roasting vegetables is another acceptable method of cooking. It is better to bake with a lid on the vegetables when possible because this allows the vegetables to cook in their own juices.

Eat vegetables with the skins left on because this provides more fiber, nutrients and flavor. Also, freshly cooked vegetables should be consumed after cooking. They lose valuable nutrients when served as leftovers or re-heated.

The Cleanse Cookbook

About Asparagus
by Christine Dreher, San Diego, CA

Selection:

Select asparagus tips that are purplish in color and have closed, compact tips. If the tips are open or soft, this is an indication that they are not fresh. The spears should be bright green in color, smooth and firm. Also, asparagus that has a strong odor is not as fresh.

Storage:

Be sure to refrigerate the asparagus as soon as possible, wrapped loosely in plastic, with the stem ends wrapped in a moist paper towel. Eat the asparagus within a few days because it does not keep long.

Preparation:

Snap off the tough white parts by bending each stem at the point where it breaks. It's also a good idea to cut off the very end of the tips because dirt gets lodged in there. Then trim the asparagus stems so that all the spears are the same length. This makes it easier to cook the asparagus uniformly. Also, if some of the spears are thicker than others, you may want to cut the thicker spears lengthwise, so that they all require the same cooking time, or start cooking the thicker spears first. Cooking time varies with the size of the spears. For smaller, more tender spears, allow 8 to 12 minutes. And for larger, thicker spears, allow 12 to 18 minutes. Do not overcook! The stalks should be tender but not limp.

To steam asparagus, you can tie the asparagus in bundles, setting them in a tall pan, with just the bottom of the stalks immersed in water, so that the tips steam, since tips take less time to cook. Cook covered with a lid or, if the asparagus is too tall, you can cover the pan with aluminum foil. You can also use a traditional metal vegetable steamer, or there are pans made just for cooking asparagus that are deep and tall, so the stalks can stand up.

Serving Suggestions:

Asparagus can be prepared a number of ways, either served hot or cooled, tossed with herbs and extra virgin olive oil or flax seed oil, or dipped in sauces. See the recipes in this section or try the "New Potatoes and Asparagus Salad" in the Salad section or the grain relish "Asparagus and Thyme Salsa" in the Grains section.

Asparagus Toss
by Christine Dreher, San Diego, CA

12 asparagus spears, cleaned and trimmed
1 1/2 Tbs. extra virgin olive oil or flax seed oil
1 Tbs. lemon juice, fresh squeezed
2 Tbs. fresh tarragon, chopped

Cook the asparagus as described in "About Asparagus" in this section entitled ." Slice the asparagus into 1-inch diagonal slices. Place in a serving bowl and toss in the remaining ingredients and serve. Makes 2 main servings or 4 side servings.

Option 1: Try minced garlic and fresh grated ginger with oil instead of tarragon and lemon juice.

Option 2: Try 2 Tbs. fresh chopped chives, 1 clove minced garlic, and 1 Tbs. fresh parsley chopped and mixed with the lemon juice oil.

Asparagus Roasted
with Lemon, Chili, and Garlic
by Sharna Gross, San Diego, CA

20 spears of asparagus
2 Tbs. lemon juice, freshly squeezed
2 Tbs. extra virgin olive oil or flax seed oil
Zest from 2 lemons (finely grated lemon peel)
1 tsp. garlic, peeled and chopped
1 tsp. chili flakes
1 Tbs. parsley, chopped
1 Tbs. raw, sprouted seeds, chopped (sunflower or
    garbanzo)

See "About Asparagus" in this section for more
information.

Preheat oven to 400°.

Roast the asparagus in a baking pan in a single layer until
light brown and soft. Remove from the oven and set aside
on a serving platter to cool to room temperature.

Combine the lemon juice, oil and garlic. Blend well and
pour on top of the asparagus.

Then mix together the zest, chili flakes, chopped raw
seeds, and parsley. Keep dry and sprinkle over the
asparagus. Serve at room temperature. Serves 4.

About Artichokes (Globe Artichokes)
by Christine Dreher, San Diego, CA

Selection:

Artichokes are in season mostly in the spring and summer. Select artichokes that feel solid and thick, that have tightly closed leaves and are olive green in color (unless it is a winter crop, which may have a brownish tinted exterior). Stay away from artichokes that have a soft consistency or leaves that are starting to open or curl. I was told about the "squeak test," which is to hold the artichoke up to you ear and squeeze it; if it squeaks, it is still fresh. Allow one medium to one large artichoke per serving.

Storage:

Store in the refrigerator unwashed, wrapped tightly in a closed plastic bag to prevent them from drying out. They will keep for about a week.

Preparation:

Artichokes can be tricky to prepare because they require trimming and cutting, but well worth the effort. For the smaller, younger artichokes that were picked before the choke developed, the only preparation for cooking needed is to be washed and trimmed at the stem.

The larger, matured artichokes need to be washed and, if preparing more than one at a time, it is a good idea to place the artichokes in 3 Tbs. of apple cider vinegar to one quart of water to prevent discoloration of the artichokes. When cut artichokes are exposed to air they can darken. Also, do not use carbon steel knives or cast iron when preparing artichokes because this causes discoloration and a metallic taste. Cut the top leaves off from the top of the artichoke (about one inch), then cut the stem even with the base of the artichoke, so that it will sit upright when

Vegetables

serving. Snip off the prickly leaf tops with a pair of scissors.

To steam artichokes (round artichokes work best for steaming), add about one inch of water in the bottom of a cooking pan with about 2 Tbs. of lemon juice to help prevent discoloration. Either stand the artichokes in the pan or use a vegetable steamer. Cover the pan, bring to a boil and reduce heat to medium-low. Cooking time varies depending on the size of the artichokes and the number. The smaller, younger artichokes can take as little as 15 minutes and the larger artichokes can take anywhere from 25 to 45 minutes. Check tenderness by inserting a knife in the bottom of the artichoke; if it inserts easily then it is ready. Or pull off a leaf; if it comes off easily, then the artichoke is ready. If not ready, recheck every few minutes. After steaming, place upside down in a colander to drain.

Serving Suggestions:

On the fully developed artichokes, only the heart and the tender meat attached to the leaves can be eaten. The choke and leaves should be discarded. To eat, pull off one leaf at a time and dip the light green, tender, meaty end into your favorite dipping sauce or herbal dressing (see the Sauces & Dips and Dressings section for ideas); pull off the tender part between your teeth, discarding the leaf. After all the leaves have been removed, you can remove the choke with a spoon; remove the inside leaves and the stem. The remaining base part is called the heart and can be eaten with a fork.

Artichokes can be eaten cold or hot. They can be used for dipping or the meat can be scraped from the leaves and pureed for soups or sauces. The artichoke hearts can be added to dishes and salads. See the recipes in this section for ideas or try the "Marinated Herb and Garlic Artichoke Dip" in the Sauces and Dips section.

Artichokes
by Angela Green

1 or 2 artichokes
2 tsp. apple cider vinegar
1 handful of fresh basil, crushed
3 cloves of garlic, peeled and sliced thin

See "About Artichokes" in this section for more information.

Cut off the pointed leaves and the top of the artichoke. Remove the stem and peel the sides. Stuff slivers of raw garlic deep between the leaves.

Fill a saucepan with about two inches of water and bring to a slow simmer. Add 1 tsp. of apple cider vinegar and some crushed basil. Place the artichoke in water.

Cover and simmer 20 to 40 minutes depending on the size and number of artichokes. When tender, but not mushy, serve with garlic lemon dip (see the Sauces and Dips section).

About Beets
by Christine Dreher, San Diego, CA

Selection:

Beets are available all year round. Select small beets that
are deep red in color and have smooth skins and firm,
slender roots. The tops should be fresh and green. The
baby beets are the sweetest and tastiest and are available
in the summer. One pound of beets yields 2 to 3 servings.

Storage:

Beets will keep for up to a week in a cool place. Cut off the
beet greens, keep in a plastic bag and store in the
refrigerator. Save the beet greens to use in dishes such as
salads and other greens dishes, preparing like spinach.
Also, you can use the beet greens in the "Vegetable Stock"
recipe in the Soups section.

Preparation:

Remove the leafy tops, leaving about one inch of stems
above the root crown. Do not trim the root ends unless the
recipe calls for this. Rinse. Being careful not to break the
skins or the beet juice will leak, causing loss of color
during cooking. Gently scrub the roots with a vegetable
brush.

To cook, boil in water for 20 to 60 minutes, depending on
the size and quantity. To test for tenderness, spoon a beet
from the pan; if the peel slides off easily, then it is ready.
Drain and cool quickly by running under water, then
remove the skins. Beets can also be baked by wrapping
them in foil, in the same manner as baked potatoes.

Serving Suggestions:

Beets can be served in a number of ways, such as sliced,
shredded or diced. Beets are great in salads and relishes or
served warm in a herbed vinaigrette dressing (see the
Dressings section for suggestions). Beets are also good in
soups and cooked with other vegetables. See the beet
recipes in this section or try the "Beet Salad" in the Salads
section or the "Beet Borsht Soup" in the Soups section.

Baked Beet Salad
by Christine Dreher, San Diego, CA

1 lb. large beets
2 to 4 Tbs. extra virgin olive oil or flax seed oil
1/2 tbs. apple cider vinegar
1 clove garlic, peeled and crushed
1 Tbs. fennel, grated
1 large onion, peeled and coarsely chopped
1 tsp. lemon juice, freshly squeezed
Dulse or vegetable seasoning, to taste (see "Seasoning
        and Flavoring Foods" in the Introduction)
2 Tbs. chives or parsley, as garnish
Cayenne pepper, to taste (optional)

See "About Beets" in this section for more information.

Preheat Oven to 350°.

Rinse and trim the beets then wrap in foil. Place in a preheated oven and bake for about 50 to 60 minutes until they are tender, testing with a fork or knife. Peel the beets while they are still warm.

Julienne the beets (cut them into thin strips). Then mix together the oil, vinegar, lemon juice, dulse, or vegetable seasoning and optional cayenne. Pour over the beets.

Dry sauté the fennel, onions, and garlic until the onions have browned slightly. Add the fennel, onions, and garlic to the beet mixture and toss gently. Add cayenne pepper if desired. Garnish with the chives or parsley. Serves 2 to 4.

Beets
with Mint, Fennel, and Red Onions
by Sharna Gross, San Diego, CA

4 large beets
1/4 cup fennel, julienne-sliced
1 Tbs. fresh mint, chopped coarsely
1/4 cup red onion, peeled and sliced thin
2 Tbs. lemon juice, freshly squeezed
2 to 4 Tbs. extra virgin olive oil or flax seed oil

See "About Beets" in this section for more information.

Cook the beets in water until tender, then cool them.

While waiting for the beets to cool, prepare the marinade. In a separate bowl combine the rest of the ingredients and marinate for a few minutes, so that the flavors can marry.

When the beets have cooled, peel and slice them into half moon shapes. Combine the beets with the marinade and serve as a cool vegetable salad. Serves 4.

About Broccoli
by Christine Dreher, San Diego, CA

Selection:

Select broccoli with small, tight, compact buds and firm stalks. Stay away from broccoli that is turning yellow, is limp or has buds opening. There are different varieties of broccoli, including purple broccoli with small clusters of purple florets; there are white and green varieties and calabrese, which is an Italian broccoli that has large flowered heads.

Storage:

Wrap in plastic bags loosely and refrigerate right away. It will stay fresh for about 5 to 7 days.

Preparation:

Cut off the tougher, bottom part of the stalk. The heads take less time to cook than the stalks, so the stalks should be cooked first. Be sure to cut thicker stalks into smaller pieces, so that the broccoli will cook evenly. Steaming in a vegetable steamer takes about 5 to 7 minutes. Do not overcook; the broccoli should be tender but not limp. I usually undercook it a little for a crisper texture. After steaming, immediately remove the broccoli from the steaming pot because the steam will continue to cook the broccoli.

Serving Suggestions:

Broccoli can be eaten raw in salads, marinated or served with dips. It can be steamed, sautéed or added to casseroles or soups. See the broccoli recipes in this section for more ideas.

Basic Broccoli
by Christine Dreher, San Diego, CA

2 cups of broccoli, steamed
1 clove garlic, peeled and crushed
2 Tbs. fresh thyme
1/8 to 1/4 cup extra virgin olive oil or flax seed oil

See "About Broccoli" in this section for more information.

Mix the garlic, thyme, and oil. Place the steamed broccoli in a serving dish and slowly toss in the oil mixture to desired quantity. Serves 2.

Note: Experiment with different herbs. Try using oregano instead of thyme for more of an Italian flavor, or add a little vegetable seasoning (see "Seasoning and Flavoring Foods" in the Introduction).

Broccoli and Cauliflower Salad
by Christine Dreher, San Diego, CA

1/4 cup sprouted sunflower seeds
1 lb. broccoli, steamed
1 lb. cauliflower, steamed
1 cup herbal vinaigrette (see Dressings section)
Cayenne pepper, to taste
1/2 tsp. paprika (garnish)
1 garlic clove, peeled and crushed (optional)

Place the steamed vegetables in a serving bowl and toss in
the herbal vinaigrette, the cayenne pepper (go easy), the
sprouted sunflower seeds, and the optional garlic. Sprinkle
the paprika on top of the salad for color. Serves 4 to 6.

About Carrots
by Christine Dreher, San Diego, CA

Selection:

Carrots should be firm and smooth and have a bright orange color. Avoid carrots that are limp or that have sprouts on their tops. Fresh-looking greens on their tops is a good indication the carrots are fresh.

Storage:

Cut off the green tops and store in plastic bags in the refrigerator. Carrots will keep about two weeks, depending on freshness.

Preparation:

Wash the carrots well and scrape off skin areas that look old. Carrots can be eaten raw in salads or sliced for dips. They can also be steamed in a vegetable steamer pan for 7 to 8 minutes until tender or can be used in soups and stir frys.

Serving Suggestions:

Adding carrots to recipes is a natural way to sweeten the flavor of the dish. It is also very good pureed in soups. Carrots can be added to soups or stir frys or steamed and tossed with an herb dressing. They can also be eaten raw in salads or served sliced with vegetable dips. See other carrot recipes in this section or try the "Carrot Ginger Soup" recipe in the Soups section or the "Candied Carrots and Apples" in the Desserts section.

Carrot Stuffing (Raw)
by Jamey Dina, N.D. and Kim Sproul, N.D., Escondido, CA
From their cookbook <u>Uncooking with Jamey & Kim</u>

2 cups carrot pulp (from juiced carrots)
3 stalks celery
3 tomatoes (vine-ripened, low-acid)
1 small purple onion, peeled
2 scallions or green onions
1/2 cup lemon juice, freshly squeezed
3/4 tsp. dried oregano
Vegetable Power or Tomato Power (see "Seasoning and
    Flavoring Foods" in the Introduction)
Whole bell peppers or tomatoes (vine-ripened, low-acid)
    to stuff; or nori sheets to roll the stuffing in; or a
    dressing or sauce (see Sauces and Dips or
    Dressings section) to top with (optional)

Finely chop or dice the celery, tomatoes, purple onion and
scallions or green onions. Combine with the carrot pulp,
lemon juice and seasonings. Hand-stir until thoroughly
mixed.

Top the stuffing with dressing or sauce, or stuff into
hollowed-out tomatoes or bell peppers, or roll in nori
sheets, or serve as-is. This is also good simply topped with
flax seed oil.

Chilled Marinated Carrots
by Christine Dreher, San Diego, CA

1 lb. carrots, sliced diagonally
1 Tbs. extra virgin olive oil or flax seed oil
2 Tbs. apple cider vinegar
1 tbs. lemon juice, freshly squeezed
1 1/2 tbs. fresh dill, minced
1 Tbs. fresh mint, minced
1 tsp. dulse, (see "Seasoning and Flavoring Foods" in
      the Introduction)

See "About Carrots" in this section for more information.

Steam the carrots in a steamer until tender, about 8
minutes. While the carrots are steaming, mix the
remaining ingredients in a large serving bowl. When the
carrots are done, place them in the serving bowl with the
remaining ingredients and toss together. Chill in the
refrigerator for at least one hour or more. Serves 2 to 4.

Sweet and Sour Carrot Medley
by Christine Dreher, San Diego, CA

1 lb. zucchini squash, julienne-sliced
3 carrots, julienne-sliced
1 red pepper, cored and julienne-sliced
3 Tbs. apple cider vinegar
2 Tbs. extra virgin olive oil or flax seed oil
2 tsp. maple syrup (or stevia to taste)
Cayenne pepper, to taste

Mix the vinegar, oil and stevia or maple syrup in a large salad bowl. Slowly add the cayenne pepper, to taste. If the mixture is not sweet enough for your taste, add more stevia or maple syrup. It should taste like a sweet and sour sauce. If you want it tangier, add a little extra apple cider vinegar.

Add the vegetables to the salad bowl and toss all the ingredients together. Cover and chill in the refrigerator for at least one hour. Serves 4.

About Corn
by Christine Dreher, San Diego, CA

Selection:

Allow one to two ears of corn per serving. Corn is in season in the summer and fall. The fresher the corn, the sweeter. Select cobs that have a green husk and silk ends. Check the kernels to make sure they are plump and have bright, cream-colored kernels. Stay away from the dark yellow colored corn because it is not usually as fresh.

Storage:

Wrap unwashed in plastic bags, leaving the husks on to keep it fresh. Store in the refrigerator. Corn will only stay fresh a few days.

Preparation:

Peel away the husks and remove the silk by rubbing under water or use a vegetable brush. To use just the kernels, remove the corn kernels from the cob by standing the corn on its end, with the flat side down. Use a sharp knife, holding the corn at its tip and cutting downward as close to the cob as possible. Scrape the cob to remove the corn pulp and milk if you want it juicier.

Serving Suggestions:

Corn can be eaten raw or cooked. The raw kernels can be added to salads. To cook, steam or boil for 7 to 10 minutes until tender; the older corn takes longer. Two ears of corn generally yield about one cup of kernels. Corn is a great addition to soups and relishes. It is also good wrapped in foil, brushed lightly with extra virgin olive oil or flax seed oil and barbecued in coals for about 15 minutes or baked, wrapped in foil, at 350° for 20 to 30 minutes. Steamed corn, brushed with extra virgin olive oil or flax seed oil and fresh tarragon, oregano, basil or chili powder, is delicious. See the corn recipes in this chapter or try the "Avocado Corn Soup (Raw)" in the Soups section or the "Corn Salad with Steamed and Dressed Asparagus" in the Salads section.

Corn on the Cob (Raw)

by Jamey Dina, N.D. and Kim Sproul, N.D., Escondido, CA
From their cookbook <u>Un</u>cooking with Jamey & Kim

Whole, raw corn (one to two ears per serving)
Unheated flax seed oil or extra virgin olive oil
Desired seasonings (see "Seasoning and Flavoring
  Foods" in the Introduction)

You do not have to cook the corn; you can eat it raw! Coat
the corn with oil in place of melted butter. Be sure not to
heat the oil. Sprinkle with herbs, such as garlic powder, or
other vegetable seasonings, if desired. This is quick, easy,
healthy and tasty!

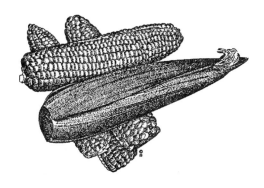

Mexican Corn Mix
by Christine Dreher, San Diego, CA

2 cups fresh corn kernels (about 4 to 5 ears of corn)
1 red pepper, diced
1 green pepper, diced
1 large Bermuda onion or 2 smaller white or yellow
    onions, peeled and diced
1 cup fresh lima beans
1 cup fresh peas
1 cup fresh carrots, shredded
2 Tbs. extra virgin olive oil or flax seed oil, with one
    garlic clove, peeled and crushed, mixed in the oil
Cayenne pepper, to taste
1 tsp. dulse or other vegetable seasoning (see
    "Seasoning and Flavoring Foods" in the
    Introduction)
2 Tbs. fresh basil, chopped
1 tsp. lemon juice, freshly squeezed

See "About Corn" in this section for more information.

Dry sauté all the seasonings and vegetables, except carrots, with the lemon juice over medium heat. Cook until the vegetables are slightly tender, 5 to 7 minutes. Add the carrots and continue to sauté for one more minute or so. Remove from the heat and add one tablespoon of the oil and then toss. Add the remaining oil, if desired. Serve hot. Serves 4.

Summer Corn Salad
by Sherry Baquial, San Diego, CA

6 ears of corn
1/8 to 1/4 cup extra virgin olive oil or flax seed oil
1 Tbs. lemon juice, freshly squeezed
1/4 large red onion, peeled and coarsely chopped
1 cucumber, coarsely chopped
1/4 cup fresh cilantro, chopped
Vegetable seasoning, to taste (see "Seasoning and
Flavoring Foods" in the Introduction)

See "About Corn" in this section for more information.

Lightly steam the corn on the cob until tender. Cool and cut the corn kernels off the cob. Mix all the ingredients together, adding the vegetable seasoning last, to taste. Serves 2 to 4.

Note: You can also use raw corn for this dish.

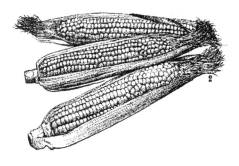

About Dulse and Kelp
by Jamey Dina, N.D. and Kim Sproul, N.D., Escondido, CA
From their cookbook <u>Un</u>cooking with Jamey & Kim

These are both types of sea vegetables and are very nutritious. They add a nice flavor and texture to salads, soups, etc. Add them to any meal for extra flavor, texture and nutrition. Dulse and kelp are both extremely high in organic, absorbable minerals, trace minerals, chlorophyll, etc.

They are available sundried in the seaweed section or in bulk bins at many health food stores, or you can prepare them yourself. Before eating, check the leaves to make sure there are no shells or other sea sediments left on them. Then rinse and soak them in purified water for 10 to 15 minutes to soften and remove the sea salt. Drain off soak water and re-rinse. The tough stem part of the kelp may be sliced into noodles.

Note from Christine: Some sea vegetables are salty in taste, which is why they make good salt substitutes, including kelp (dulse) and bladderwrack. Some are sweeter like kombu, sea palm and wakame. Some are tangy, including nori (used for sushi rolls), arame and hikiki. They can be used in soups, sauces or in salads.

About Eggplant
by Christine Dreher, San Diego, CA

Selection:

There are different varieties of eggplant, varying in shape and color. Some are long and thin, while others are round or pear-shaped. Most eggplant are purplish-black in color, but some are yellow, white or green. Allow about one medium size eggplant, or 1 1/2 pounds, for two main servings or four side servings. Select eggplant that feel heavy, with a shiny, smooth skin. They are usually available all year.

Storage:

Keep in a cool place or refrigerate up to 3 days.

Preparation:

Be sure to use a stainless steel knife when cutting to prevent discoloration of the eggplant. Rinse and trim off the tops, but do not remove the peeling. Eggplant can be steamed, broiled, sautéed, baked or grilled. To bake eggplant, place the eggplant on a baking sheet and bake at 400° for 45 to 50 minutes. Cut in half and drain. To puree, scoop out the insides and puree in a blender. See the "Eggplant Dip with Cilantro, Cumin and Red Peppers" recipe in the Sauces and Dips section.

Serving Suggestions:

Eggplant can be stir-fried with other vegetables. It can also be baked in slices and covered with a fresh tomato sauce or baked and tossed with oil and fresh herbs. See the "Ratatouille" or "Baked Eggplant with Cumin" recipes, which are both in this section.

Baked Eggplant
with Cumin
by Ivi Turner, San Diego, CA

2 lbs. Japanese eggplant, cleaned
6 cloves garlic, peeled and chopped fine
1 tsp. paprika
1 1/2 tsp. ground cumin
Dash of cayenne pepper
Dulse or vegetable seasoning, to taste (see "Seasoning
     and Flavoring Foods" in the Introduction)
Juice of 1 lemon

See "About Eggplant" in this section for more information.

Preheat oven to 450°.

Slit the skin of the eggplants in several places, place on a
baking sheet and cook in the oven for 35 to 40 minutes.
Cool and slice lengthwise into three pieces. Sprinkle with
garlic.

Place the eggplant slices in a non-stick roasting dish and
sprinkle with cumin, paprika, cayenne and dulse, or
vegetable seasoning. Bake for 5 to 8 minutes. Remove from
the heat and sprinkle with lemon juice before serving.
Serves 4.

About Jerusalem Artichokes
by Christine Dreher, San Diego, CA

Selection:

Jerusalem artichokes resemble bumpy, new potatoes or ginger root. There are two varieties: light brown and red. The light brown are easier to find and have more flavor. They are similar to water chestnuts in texture. Select firm artichokes because they get softer and wrinkled when they get old. Allow 1 1/2 pounds for four servings.

Storage:

Store in a cool, dark and dry place or place in plastic bags and refrigerate. They will keep for a week or longer.

Preparation:

Scrub well with a vegetable brush and steam or boil with the peelings intact for about 10 minutes. They can also be baked like a potato, with the skins on, for about 30 to 35 minutes. Peel after cooking. It makes it much easier to eat.

Serving Suggestions:

Jerusalem artichokes can be eaten raw or cooked. To eat raw, peel and grate or slice them and toss them with a little fresh lemon juice to prevent discoloration. They can be added to salads or dipped in sauces. Steamed and sliced Jerusalem artichokes are good tossed with fresh lemon juice, oil and fresh garlic and parsley. They are also good pureed in soups. See the Jerusalem artichoke recipes in this section or try the "Jerusalem Artichokes and Onion Soup" recipe in the Soups section.

Italian Style Jerusalem Artichokes
by Christine Dreher, San Diego, CA

1 1/2 lbs. Jerusalem artichokes, scrubbed
1 lb. tomatoes (vine-ripened, low-acid), peeled, de-
    seeded, and diced
1 Tbs. vegetable seasoning (see "Seasoning and
    Flavoring Foods" in the Introduction)
1 tsp. dulse or other salt substitute
1 Tbs. extra virgin olive oil or flax seed oil
1 clove garlic, peeled and crushed
1 Tbs. fresh oregano, chopped
1 Tbs. fresh basil, chopped
2 Tbs. fresh parsley, minced, for garnish
1 tsp. lemon juice, freshly squeezed

See "About Jerusalem Artichokes" in this section for more
information.

Clean and scrub the Jerusalem artichokes, steaming or
boiling them in water for 5 to 6 minutes. Drain, peel and
dice.

In a saucepan, dry sauté the garlic, dulse, oregano, basil
and lemon juice until the garlic is slightly browned. Add
the tomatoes and vegetable seasoning, then cover and
simmer on low heat for about 10 minutes. Remove from
the heat and mix in the Jerusalem artichokes and oil. Place
in a serving bowl and sprinkle the parsley on top. Serves 3
to 6.

Jerusalem Artichokes O'Brien
by Christine Dreher, San Diego, CA

1 lb. Jerusalem artichokes
Juice of one lemon
1 Tbs. or more of extra virgin olive oil or flax seed oil
1 red onion, peeled and sliced
1 red pepper, chopped
1 green pepper, chopped
1 garlic clove, peeled and crushed
Dulse, to taste
Vegetable seasoning, to taste (see "Seasoning and
     Flavoring Foods" in the Introduction)
2 Tbs. fresh parsley, chopped for garnish
Cayenne pepper, to taste (optional)

See "About Jerusalem Artichokes" in this section for more information.

Bring 1 quart of water and the lemon juice, except one teaspoon, to a boil in a medium-size saucepan. Add the artichokes and cook until slightly tender, about 4 to 5 minutes. Drain.

While the artichokes are cooking, dry sauté the remaining ingredients, except the parsley and oil, in the lemon juice until the onions have browned. Add the artichokes and continue sautéing for 2 to 3 more minutes. Place on a serving plate and drizzle with oil and top with garnish. Serves 2 to 4.

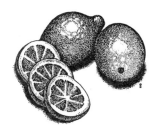

Jerusalem Artichokes and Asparagus Toss
by Christine Dreher, San Diego, CA

Lemon juice of 1 large lemon or 2 small lemons
1 lb. of asparagus, cleaned and trimmed
1/2 lb. Jerusalem artichokes, cleaned and scrubbed
2 tsp. or more extra virgin olive oil or flax seed oil
2 tsp. fresh dill
1 clove garlic, peeled and crushed
1 tsp. fresh parsley, chopped

Cook the asparagus as described on the "About Asparagus" page in this section. Cook the Jerusalem artichokes as described on the "About Jerusalem Artichokes" page in this section. Use 1/2 of the lemon juice to cook the artichokes.

Toss the artichokes with the other 1/2 of the lemon juice and the parsley. Arrange in the center of a large serving plate.

Cut the cooked asparagus into one-inch pieces, then toss the asparagus in a bowl with the oil and garlic. Arrange the asparagus on the serving plate, by placing the asparagus in a circle around the outside of the artichokes. Sprinkle the fresh dill over the entire dish. Serves 2 to 4.

About Mushrooms
by Christine Dreher, San Diego, CA

Selection:

Select fresh and firm mushrooms. Stay away from dry, wilted or slimy mushrooms. They come in buttons, cups and flat styles and can be white, brown or cream-colored. They have been freshly picked when the gills underneath are not visible or opened yet. Allow 1 pound for 4 to 6 side servings.

Storage:

Mushrooms will store in the refrigerator for up to a week in a paper or cloth bag. Do not store in plastic bags because this makes them sticky.

Preparation:

Wipe the mushrooms clean with a damp cloth or paper towel or put them in a colander and quickly rinse under cool water, then dry them. Do not soak in water. Trim the stalk ends. Mushrooms require little cooking time and can be eaten raw or cooked.

Serving Suggestions:

Mushrooms are good raw in salads or served with dips or marinated. They are also good dry sautéed with other vegetables, baked and stuffed, or cooked in sauces and soups. See recipes in this section for more ideas or try the "Mushroom Millet Soup" or the "Wild Mushroom Soup with Onion Puree" in the Soups section.

Smoked Mushrooms
by Ivi Turner, San Diego, CA

1 lb. mushrooms, whole or halved
1 red pepper, cut in strips
1 green pepper, cut in strips
2 yellow squash, cut in 1 inch half-moons
2 zucchini, cut in 1 inch half-moons
1 bunch fresh basil, chopped
Extra virgin olive oil or flax seed oil, to taste (optional)

Preheat broiler on top rack of oven.

Place all the vegetables on a cookie sheet and broil them on the top rack of the oven. Turn until browned on all sides. Add fresh basil and toss. Toss with small amount of oil after cooking (optional). Serve hot, room temperature, or cold. Serves 2.

Stuffed Mushrooms
by Jacque Frank, Hudson, FL

4 shiitake mushrooms
1 clove garlic, peeled and chopped
1 avocado, peeled and quartered
1/4 tsp. cumin
1 tomato (vine-ripened, low-acid)
1/4 tsp. coriander
1/4 tsp. lemon or lime juice
3 Tbs. onion, peeled and grated
1/2 tsp. of curry powder, to taste, or your favorite
          vegetable seasoning (see "Seasoning and
          Flavoring Foods" in the Introduction)

See "About Mushrooms" in this section for more information.

Blend the avocado, lemon juice, garlic, cumin, coriander, curry powder or vegetable seasoning, in a blender until creamy. If it is too thick, add a little water. Chop the tomato into small pieces and add it to the avocado mix.

Lightly steam the mushroom caps; remove them from the heat and sprinkle them with a dash of curry powder. Stuff the mushrooms with the avocado mix and top with grated onions. Serves 2.

Vegetable Medley
with Roasted Mushrooms
by Christine Dreher, San Diego, CA

2 lbs. broccoli crowns
2 lbs. fresh mushrooms
3 large carrots, sliced
1 large red onion, peeled and coarsely chopped
1 red pepper, cored and coarsely chopped
3 Tbs. fresh thyme, chopped
1 Tbs. dulse or vegetable seasoning (see "Seasoning and
       Flavoring Foods" in the Introduction)
2 to 4 Tbs. extra virgin olive oil or flax seed oil
1/4 cup lemon juice, freshly squeezed
2 tsp. fresh oregano, chopped
1 Tbs. fresh parsley, chopped
1 clove garlic, peeled and crushed

Preheat oven to 250°

See "About Mushrooms," "About Carrots," and "About Broccoli" in this section for more information.

Place the cleaned mushrooms, red peppers, and onions in a large baking dish. Add the lemon juice, dulse, thyme, oregano, and garlic. Toss the mixture and spread evenly in the pan. Roast for 20 to 30 minutes until the mushrooms and onions are tender.

While the mushrooms and onions are roasting, steam the carrots for 3 to 4 minutes and then add the broccoli to the carrots. Continue steaming for 4 to 5 minutes, until the vegetables are tender. When the mushroom mixture is done, remove it from the oven and place it in a serving dish with the broccoli and carrots. Toss in the oil and parsley. You may want to add a little fresh lemon juice for zest. Serve immediately. Serves 4.

Note: You can save the stalks for the "Broccomole" recipe in the Sauces and Dips section.

About Parsnips
by Christine Dreher, San Diego, CA

Selection:

Parsnips are loaded with fiber. They look like a whitish carrot. Select parsnips that are small to medium in size because the larger parsnips can be tougher. The color should be a creamy white and have a smooth, firm texture. The roots should be firm and well-shaped. One pound of parsnips yields four servings.

Storage:

Keep parsnips refrigerated in plastic bags. They will keep for a week or two.

Preparation:

To cook parsnips, scrub them in cold water, then trim off the top and the root ends. Steam in a covered pot with a vegetable steamer for about 15 minutes, depending on the size. Do not overcook because they can become mushy. Drain well and, to dry them, return them to the pan and cook on low for a few minutes. Parsnips can also be cooked in vegetable broth (see "Vegetable Broth" recipe in the Soups section) or they can be baked like a potato, wrapped in foil, for about 45 minutes.

Serving Suggestions:

Parsnips can be eaten raw, shredded in salads or marinated with other raw vegetables. They can be cooked with other vegetables or tossed with oil and fresh herbs. They can be steamed or baked and served with one of the sauces from the Sauces section. They can also be mashed like potatoes, blending in your favorite sauce. Adding a little stevia, maple syrup, or honey enhances their naturally sweet flavor. See the parsnip recipes in this section for more ideas.

Cooked Parsnips
with Herbed Vegetable Broth
by Christine Dreher, San Diego, CA

6 to 7 parsnips
Juice of 1 lemon
Dulse or other salt substitute, to taste
1 cup vegetable stock (see Soups section)
1 Tbs. vegetable seasoning (see "Seasoning and
Flavoring Foods" in the Introduction)
1 tsp. fresh chives
1 tsp. fresh dill
1 tsp. fresh parsley
1 tsp. fresh thyme
1 Tbs. extra virgin olive oil or flax seed oil (optional)

See "About Parsnips" in this section for more information.

Clean and trim the parsnips, cutting them into bite-size cubes. Place the lemon juice, vegetable stock, vegetable seasoning, and dulse into a saucepan, bringing to a boil. Add the parsnips and herbs. Cook, uncovered, for about 15 minutes, until the parsnips are tender. Remove from the heat. Oil can be added if desired. Serve hot. Serves 3 to 4.

Roasted Parsnips
with Maple and Rosemary
by Sharna Gross, San Diego, CA

8 parsnips, peeled and sliced
1 Tbs. fresh rosemary, chopped
1/4 cup maple syrup
1/4 cup vegetable stock (see Soups section)

See "About Parsnips" in this section for more information.

Dry sauté the parsnips until half cooked. Add the maple syrup and vegetable stock and boil until the liquid is reduced to a coating on the parsnips and the parsnips are soft. Toss in the rosemary and serve. Makes 4 cups.

Rosemary

About Potatoes
by Christine Dreher, San Diego, CA

Selection:

There are basically two types of potatoes, including the thin skinned (new potatoes), which are good for salads, sautéing and boiling, and thick skinned (mature potatoes) which are good for baking, roasting and pureeing. Select potatoes that have somewhat smooth skins and are free of blemishes. Stay away from potatoes that are soft or have sprouts growing. With new potatoes, they are fresh if the skin rubs off easily. Allow 1 baking potato per serving or 3 new potatoes.

Storage:

Keep potatoes in a cool, dry, dark, well ventilated place and do not leave them in plastic bags because this will make them rot. They can keep for a month or longer.

Preparation:

Scrub potatoes well with a vegetable brush under running water. Steam or boil the new potatoes in their skins for about 10 to 15 minutes until they are tender. For mature potatoes, steam or boil in chunks for about 20 to 25 minutes until tender. Drain and dry before using. To bake potatoes, rub the skin lightly with oil and pierce the skin with a fork in several places to allow the steam to escape. Bake in a preheated oven at 450° for about 45 minutes or longer until tender.

Serving Suggestions:

Potatoes are good steamed, boiled or baked, then tossed with oil and fresh herbs, such as dill weed, chives, parsley or curry powder. See recipes in this section or try the "New Potato and Asparagus Salad" in the Salads section or the "Potato Leek Soup" in the Soups section.

Roasted Red Potatoes
with Rosemary
by Ivi Turner, San Diego, CA

8 to 10 medium red potatoes
1 bunch fresh rosemary
Dulse, to taste
Juice of 1 lemon

Preheat oven to 400°.

See "About Potatoes" in this section for more information.

Cut the potatoes into bite-size wedges. Toss with dulse and lemon juice. Bake in a preheated oven until done, approximately 45 minutes, turning once. Just before the potatoes are done, sprinkle them with rosemary and continue baking for 5 minutes. Serves 4 to 5.

Option: Brush lightly with extra virgin olive oil before or after cooking or flax seed oil after cooking.

Stuffed Baked Potatoes
with Vegetable Stuffing
by Sharna Gross, San Diego, CA

4 large baking potatoes, baked and cooled

1st Portion Filling

Dice the following cleaned vegetables into 1/4 inch-chunks.

1 carrot	**10 mushrooms**
1/4 cup zucchini	**1/4 cup broccoli**
1/4 cup chopped onion,	**1/4 cup asparagus tips**
peeled	

2nd Portion Filling

1 clove garlic	**1/2 cup fresh parsley**
1/2 cup fresh basil	**1 cup extra virgin olive oil**
1 cup fresh spinach	**or flax seed oil**
2 Tbs. lemon juice, freshly	
squeezed	

Preheat oven to 350°.

See "About Potatoes" in this section for more information.

Slice the baked potatoes in half, lengthwise, and scoop out the potato, leaving the skin intact. Set aside the potato and the potato shells. Then dry sauté the ingredients from the 1st portion filling until golden colored and soft. Then blend the 2nd portion filling ingredients in a blender until pureed. You may add more oil, if needed, for a smoother texture.

Mix in the scooped out potatoes with the blended 2nd portion filling. Then fold in the 1st portion filling. Place the mixture back into the potato skins and bake in a 350° oven until heated all the way through. Serves 4.

About Squash
by Christine Dreher, San Diego, CA

Winter Varieties

Selection:

Winter varieties include: butternut (yellowish, pear-shaped, elongated), hubbard (large, green), acorn (dark green, shaped like a big acorn), spaghetti squash (yellow, large, melon shaped), pumpkin (orange, round). The winter squash is usually larger than the summer squash with thicker, harder skins that may or may not need to be peeled before cooking. The pulp should be thick and bright yellow or orange in color.

Storage:

Winter squash will keep for up to a month or longer in a dry, cool place.

Preparation:

You may need a heavy-bladed knife or hand saw to cut the winter squash. Cut in half or in wedges, then de-seed and remove the stringy flesh from the inside. It can be baked with a little stevia or maple syrup in a pre-heated oven at 375° for 30 to 45 minutes, depending on its size. It can also be cut in chunks and steamed (steam for about 10 minutes for one-inch cubes) or boiled. Spaghetti squash is baked whole with the skin on and then cut in half, with the stringy fibers removed before serving.

Serving Suggestions:

Winter squash can be cooked with stevia or maple syrup, coriander, allspice, or nutmeg. See the squash recipes in this section, including "Mock Spaghetti" and "Spaghetti Squash with Herbs" or try the "Golden Squash Soup" in the Soups section or the "Stuffed Acorn Squash" in the Grains section.

Vegetables

Summer Varieties

Selection:

Summer varieties include: zucchini (dark green, oblong shaped, also green-striped or yellow), crookneck (orange or yellow), chayote (green, pear-shaped), patty pan (light or dark green in color), cymling (scallop-shaped, orange), custard marrow (color varies from light to dark green with strips, or yellow, round). The summer squash is thinner skinned and usually requires no peeling. Select squash that has a fresh, glossy and smooth skin and is heavy for its size. One pound of squash provides about 3 to 4 side servings or 2 main servings.

Storage:

Summer squash should be stored in a plastic bag in the refrigerator for up to one week.

Preparation:

Wash the squash with a vegetable brush and trim the top and remove the stem ends. Do not peel before cooking. Cut into pieces or cook whole. Steam in a vegetable steamer. Do not overcook because squash will become mushy. When cooking zucchini, it should be tender but still have a crisp texture. Squash can also be dry sautéed or baked.

Serving Suggestions:

Summer squash can be cooked with a variety of herbs including: basil, chive, dill, oregano, thyme, curry powder, parsley or garlic. Zucchini can be eaten raw by slicing or grating it into salads or cutting it in strips and serving with a vegetable dip. Summer squash is great steamed, then tossed with oil and fresh herbs. Chayote squash is very good stuffed and baked. See the recipes in this section for more ideas.

Mashed Summer Squash
by Christine Dreher, San Diego, CA

2 lbs. of patty pan or crookneck squash, diced
2 Tbs. extra virgin olive oil or flax seed oil
Your favorite herbs, to taste
**Vegetable seasoning, to taste, optional (see "Seasonings
    and Flavoring Foods" in the Introduction)**

See "About Squash - Summer Varieties" in this section for
more information.

Steam the squash until tender. Mash the squash coarsely,
adding the oil (you may want to add more) and the fresh
herbs and the optional vegetable seasoning. Serve hot.
Serves 4.

Dill

Mock Spaghetti (Raw)

by Jamey Dina, N.D. and Kim Sproul, N.D., Escondido, CA
From their cookbook <u>Uncooking with Jamey & Kim</u>

**Any summer squash (zucchini, crookneck, or
sunburst)**
Fresh-squeezed lemon juice or any sauce or dressing

See "About Squash - Summer Varieties" in this section for
more information.

Shred the squash lengthwise into long "spaghetti" strands.
Any shredding device will work. The longer the squash is,
the longer the "spaghetti" will be. Sunburst squash will
make shorter strands, more like noodles. Eat as-is, or top
with lemon juice or any sauce or dressing (see "Spaghetti
Sauce" in the Sauces and Dips section or the Dressings
sections for suggestions).

Simmered Chayote Squash
by Christine Dreher, San Diego, CA

1 1/2 lbs. chayote squash, peeled, cut in half
      lengthwise, de-seeded and sliced thin
1 Tbs. chives, chopped, for garnish
1 Tbs. extra virgin olive oil or flax seed oil
1 large shallot, chopped fine
2 cloves garlic, peeled and crushed
1 Tbs. lemon juice, freshly squeezed
3 Tbs. fresh tarragon
1/2 tsp. of dulse or other vegetable seasoning (see
      "Seasoning and Flavoring Foods" in the
      Introduction)
3 to 4 oz. of vegetable broth (see the Soups section)

See "About Squash - Summer Varieties" in this section for more information.

Over medium heat, dry sauté the shallots and garlic for about one minute. Then add the squash, tarragon, dulse and lemon juice. Stir while adding the vegetable broth. Reduce to low heat and simmer, covered, for about 8 minutes until the squash is tender. Remove from heat, add the oil, and toss.

Place in a serving bowl and sprinkle the chives on top. Serves 3 to 6.

Spaghetti Squash
with Rosemary, Chili, and Garlic
by Sharna Gross, San Diego, CA

1 large spaghetti squash
1 Tbs. rosemary, chopped
1 garlic clove, peeled and chopped
1/4 cup extra virgin olive oil or flax seed oil
1 tsp. chili flakes
2 tsp. lemon juice, freshly squeezed

Preheat oven to 350°.

See "About Squash - Winter Varieties" in this section for more information.

Cut the spaghetti squash in halves and place them face down in a baking dish. Cook in a preheated oven until tender 30 to 35 minutes (depending on size). When slightly cooled but still warm, pull the squash apart with a fork (it will resemble spaghetti). Place in a bowl and toss with the remaining ingredients. Serve. Makes 6 cups.

Mixed Vegetable Dishes

Alkalizing Sushi

by Emily Mudhar-Fung, Blackheath, London, England
option by Christine Dreher

1 small avocado
1 tomato (vine-ripened, low-acid)
1/2 green pepper
1/4 cucumber
Handful of spinach
1 tsp. mixed herbs (use your favorite vegetable seasoning
      combination; see "Seasoning and Flavoring
      Foods" in the Introduction)
3 sheets of nori sheets (dried seaweed papers)
Dash of lemon juice, freshly squeezed
1/3 cup grated carrots, for color and sweetness (optional)

Chop and mix all the above ingredients except for the nori sheets. Cut the nori sheets in half and roll the other ingredients inside the sushi sheets. Serves 2 to 4.

Option 1: Christine suggests serving the sushi with one of the sauces in the Sauces and Dips section.

Option 2: Same as above but spread a layer of cooked millet (see the Grains section and cook the millet with a little extra water to make sure it is sticky) on the nori sheets and then add the other ingredients on top and then roll. You may want to add some vegetable seasoning to the water when cooking the millet for more flavor. I also prefer using full nori sheets for this instead of half sheets.

"Confetti" Vegetable Curry
by Ivi Turner, San Diego, CA

1 cup onion, peeled and diced
1/3 cup red bell pepper, diced
1 cup sweet potato, diced
1 cup zucchini, diced
1 cup mushrooms, sliced
1 cup fresh corn, cut off cob
1/2 cup fresh shelled peas
3 large tomatoes (vine-ripened, low-acid), diced
1 Tbs. ginger root, minced
1 Tbs. curry powder
1/2 tsp. ground cumin
Juice of 1 lemon, freshly squeezed
1/4 cup vegetable broth (see recipe in Soups section)
A few tsp. tomato juice (optional)

In a non-stick large saucepan, dry sauté the onions in the lemon juice and/or a little tomato juice, stirring often, for about 10 minutes until they start to brown.

Add the minced ginger root, curry powder, and ground cumin and cook for 1 minute. Add the vegetables, except the corn, and continue to cook for 3 minutes, stirring occasionally.

Add the chopped tomatoes to the vegetables, along with the vegetable broth. Simmer, partially covered, until the vegetables are tender and the liquid has somewhat thickened, about 10-15 minutes. Remove from heat and stir in the corn. Serves 4 to 6.

Option: For a spicier curry taste, add extra curry powder.

Lettuce Sandwiches

by Jamey Dina, N.D. and Kim Sproul, N.D., Escondido, CA
From their cookbook <u>Uncooking</u> *with Jamey & Kim*

Lettuce leaves (any variety of lettuce will work, but the outer leaves will make the easiest-to-handle sandwich)
Avocado, cucumber, tomato, sprouts, carrots, or any other fillings of choice

Carefully remove three of the outer leaves. When doing so, try not to tear any part of the leaves other than what is directly attached to the head so that your sandwich will stay together and not leak if you fill it with something watery.

Use two pieces of lettuce for the bottom of your sandwich so that it will not break. Fill the lettuce with vegetables, other lettuces, or sprouts you like. Don't stack ingredients so high that you won't be able to close the sides over the filling. Some avocado may be used to stick the vegetables together.

Try using one of the dressings or sauces in the Dressings or Sauces and Dips sections. You may want to use less liquid when making dressings or sauces for use in sandwiches.

Fold the leaves over the filling and wrap the third leaf over the top of the sandwich to prevent the filling from falling out. You may need to use two hands to eat this, depending on the size of your leaves and hands.

Other varieties of lettuce cannot be stuffed as much as iceberg lettuce, but they still work well and are more nutritious. Red leaf lettuce tends to fall apart more easily than other varieties but is also more tender and, therefore, good to use as a second leaf or inside the sandwich as part of the filling. Enjoy!

Polynesian Fresh Vegetables with Herbed Millet
by Andrew & Kathleen Myler, Los Angeles, CA

Millet:

4 cups of cooked millet (see Grains section)
1 tsp. dried thyme

The Medley: Cut the following into bite-size pieces.

1 cup each of yellow, red and green bell peppers
1 cup of zucchini
1 cup of yellow squash
1/2 cup of shredded coconut
2 cups of pineapple (try apple if you don't want to mix
        citrus with vegetables)

The Dressing:

1/2 cup extra virgin olive oil or flax seed oil
1/4 cup of apple cider vinegar
1 1/2 tsp. curry powder
1 tsp. of vegetable seasoning (see "Seasoning and
        Flavoring Foods" in the Introduction)

Cook the millet. While the millet is cooking, chop the vegetables, pineapple or apple, and coconut and place them in a large bowl and set aside.

Mix the dressing ingredients, saving 2 Tbs. of the oil. Toss in the medley ingredients with the dressing.

When the millet is done, add the oil and thyme to it and mix. Place the millet on a large serving plate and cover with the medley and dressing mixture. Serves 4 to 6.

Quick Meal (Raw)
by Jamey Dina, N.D. and Kim Sproul, N.D., Escondido, CA
From their cookbook <u>Un</u>cooking with Jamey & Kim

Avocado
2 to 3 cucumbers
3 medium tomatoes (vine-ripened, low-acid)
Sprouts or greens (such as buckwheat or sunflower
greens)

Chop the first three ingredients and mix together, mashing
the avocado as you mix. The juices of the tomatoes and the
cucumbers will mix with the avocado to form an instant,
creamy dressing. The amount of avocado you use depends
on how creamy you want it. But remember, avocados are
high in fat, so don't overdo it!

Options: Serve with sprouts or greens. Be creative: mix
with any vegetables. Christine recommends using
vegetable seasoning, to taste. See "Seasoning and
Flavoring Foods" section in the Introduction for
suggestions.

Ratatouille
by Christine Dreher, San Diego, CA

1 red bell pepper, cut in large bite-size pieces
Cayenne, to taste (easy does it!)
1 1/2 cups red onion, peeled and cubed
Pinch of marjoram and rosemary
1 1/2 cups green beans, cut in bite size pieces
1 tsp. oregano, dried
4 to 5 cloves of garlic, peeled and pressed
1 tsp. thyme, dried
1 medium eggplant, peeled and cut in bite-size pieces
1 Tbs. basil, dried
2 zucchini, sliced
6 large Roma tomatoes (vine-ripened, low-acid)
2 cups of mushrooms, sliced

Dry sauté the peppers, onion, green beans, and garlic in a non-stick pan, over medium heat. Add a few drops of lemon juice to prevent the vegetables from sticking. Sauté for approximately 10 minutes until the green beans are slightly tender.

Add the eggplant, zucchini and mushrooms to the skillet. Continue to sauté 5 more minutes. Add 1/2 of the tomatoes and cover to steam.

Meanwhile, blend the remaining tomatoes and the spices in a blender or food processor. Add to the skillet and cover. Cook until desired tenderness. Serve over millet or quinoa. Serves 2 to 4.

Option: Oil can be added after cooking, if desired.

Roasted Vegetable Medley
by Ivi Turner, San Diego, CA

1 large red bell pepper
1 large green bell pepper
1 large yellow bell pepper
2 medium red onions, peeled
1 small (10 oz.) eggplant
2 medium yellow summer squash
1/8 cup Italian parsley, minced
2 Tbs. fresh thyme, minced
4 garlic cloves, peeled and halved
Dulse or vegetable seasoning, to taste (see "Seasonings
    and Flavoring Foods" in the Introduction)

Preheat oven to 400°.

Cut the vegetables into large bite-size pieces (because they
tend to shrink during cooking). In a bowl, combine the
vegetables and garlic halves with vegetable seasonings to
coat.

Spread the vegetables evenly in a large non-stick pan and
roast them in a preheated oven, turning often with a
spatula until browned and tender, about 30 to 40 minutes.
Sprinkle with parsley and thyme. Serves 2.

Sweet Potato Veggie Goulash
by Christine Dreher

5 medium to large sweet potatoes, scrubbed and cubed
3 small stalks of broccoli, sliced
3 large carrots, peeled and sliced
3 cups cut green beans, cut
5 cloves of peeled, crushed garlic
1/2 cup flax seed oil or extra virgin olive oil
Other seasonings (optional)

Combine garlic and oil in a bowl and let set. Steam sweet potatoes for about 15 minutes until soft. Remove sweet potatoes from heat, mash until smooth. Set aside 3 Tbs. of the oil and garlic mixture for the steamed vegetables. Add the sweet potatoes to the remaining garlic and oil mixture and blend together.

Steam the green beans for about 5 to 7 minutes, then add the carrots for 5 minutes, then add the broccoli for the last 5 minutes or less until tender. Remove steamed vegetables from heat and steamer and chop into small bite size pieces. Toss the vegetables with the 3 Tbs. of oil and garlic mixture set aside. Add in optional seasonings (I like the Italian seasoning combination or nutritional yeast). You can save the water from the steamed vegetables for the optional vegetable broth.

Combine the steamed vegetables with the sweet potato mixture. Mix well. If the mixture appears too thick, you can add the vegetable broth to desired texture. Serves four.

Option: Instead of using steamed vegetables, you could use your favorite raw vegetables. I like carrots, corn on the cob, broccoli, zucchini squash, red onion and red or yellow peppers to taste. Chop the broccoli, onion and peppers very fine, grate the carrots and zucchini squash and cut the corn kernels from the cob. Try the raw vegetable seasonings listed in "Seasonings" in the Resource and References Section. Mix with the sweet potato mixture and serve.

Steam-Fry Vegetables
by Mary Jane Heinrichs, Lincoln, NE
(modified by Christine Dreher)

Use your favorite vegetables for this dish. Suggestions:

Onions	**Potatoes**	**Carrots**
Celery	**Cabbage**	**Cauliflower**
Green Beans	**Broccoli**	**Zucchini**
Mushrooms	**Peppers**	

Fresh herbs
1 tsp. cayenne pepper
1/2 to 3/4 cup apple cider vinegar
Extra virgin olive oil or flax seed oil, to taste

Clean and cut the vegetables into bite-size pieces. Separate them into groups based on cooking times. For example, potatoes, carrots, celery, cabbage, cauliflower, and green beans take longer. Zucchini, mushrooms, peppers, and onions take less time.

Add the vegetables to the steamer in order of cooking time. Allow an extra 5 to 10 minutes of steaming for the longer-cooking vegetables before adding the quicker-cooking vegetables. Remove from the steamer when tender, yet crisp. Do not overcook.

Top with your favorite herbs, oil, and cayenne/apple cider vinegar. Or, mix in a shaker bottle: your favorite herbs, 1 tsp. of cayenne pepper, 1/2 to 3/4 cup of apple cider vinegar, and optionally, oil, to taste. Shake well.

Serve over millet, quinoa, or amaranth (see the Grains section). Also see "Seasoning and Flavoring Foods" in the Introduction for more seasoning ideas.

Vegetables
with Millet

by Xanthe Skjelfjord, Charlottesville, VA

1 bunch kale, stripped from stem
2 carrots, peeled and diced
1 cup millet, cooked (see Grains section)
Fresh parsley, chopped
1 bunch broccoli, florets and stems cut into julienne
         strips

Steam the vegetables minimally in shallow water with a
vegetable steamer. Put the carrots and kale in first, the
broccoli next, and the parsley last. (Christine likes to put
fresh ginger in the water as the vegetables are steaming.
Nice taste, especially with carrots!).

Serve over millet or quinoa and top with fresh lemon juice
and 1 Tbs. of oil. Add your favorite seasonings (see the
"Seasoning and Flavoring Foods" section in the
Introduction). Serves 2 to 4.

Vegetables

Grains

Grains

Information about Grains

It is important to wash grains before cooking. This removes the dust and debris and gives the grain a cleaner, sweeter taste when cooked.

Grains must be stored properly in order to maintain nutritional value and prevent spoilage due to rancidity or infestation. Store raw grains in airtight glass or ceramic jars in a cool place. Bay leaf or mint sprigs wrapped in cheesecloth can be placed in the grain containers to further ensure the proper storage environment. Several herbs, such as lavender and bay leaf, placed in your grain cabinet will help ward off moths.

Store cooked grains in the refrigerator only if cooked with vegetable broth or beans. Refrigeration will dry out cooked whole grains. Grains prepared with only water and spices can be stored at room temperature up to three days in the winter and one day in the summer. Mold usually won't appear in room-temperature grains for five days.

Note: Grains should be consumed in moderation while cleansing because too many grains can slow down the cleansing process. I recommend no more than 2 or 3 times per week. After cleansing, they can be incorporated fully into a balanced pH diet.

Grains

Types of Grains

Amaranth – It's pH is more alkaline than most grains, but more acidic than millet or quinoa. This is a tiny seed grain that is highly nutritional. It is high in protein, iron, calcium, phosphorus and vitamins C and A. It is also exceptionally rich in the essential amino acid lysine. It is low in carbohydrates and gluten. Blend amaranth with other grains in a ratio of 1:3 or 1:4 for a dish that has complete protein balance. Amaranth has a mild, sweet, nutty flavor and a gelatinous consistency, though its seeds crunch even when cooked.

Brown Rice - It's pH is more acidic than amaranth, millet, or quinoa. It should not be used during cleansing, but can be added to your diet after the cleanse process in balance with other more alkaline grains.

Millet - This is the most alkaline of the grains. This is a grain high in some B vitamins, copper and iron. It is the easiest grain to digest . When cooked millet has cooled, it has an ideal texture for molding or shaping for various dishes, such as millet burgers.

Quinoa - (pronounced "keen wa") - This is an alkalizing grain. This is a hardy grain and contains the highest amount of protein of any grain. It cooks quickly and makes a delicious, crunchy dish. It is high in calcium, phosphorus, iron, B vitamins and vitamin E and has an ideal balance of amino acids. Be sure to wash quinoa thoroughly to remove the saponin, the rust-colored coating that protects this seed against insects, birds and the sun. While cooking, the germ on the outside of the grain unfolds like a partial spiral.

Cooking Grains

When cooking grains, use a heavy pot, preferably stainless steel or porcelain, or pottery that is lead-free, and use a tightly fitting lid. Rinse the grains before cooking. Boil water and then add the grain. Return to a boil, reduce to a simmer, cover and cook for the time indicated. Once the water is absorbed, fluff with a fork and remove from the heat. Let sit for 15 minutes before serving. Keep in mind that the water proportion slightly decreases when you cook 3 or more cups of grains.

The following table provides cooking times for grains used in cleanse cooking. These times may vary, so you should start testing for tenderness about five to ten minutes before their done time and then continue to check every few minutes:

Grain	Amount	Water	Cooking Time
Amaranth	1 C	2 1/2 C	20 minutes
Millet	1 C	2 C	25 minutes
Quinoa	1 C	2 C	15 minutes
Brown Rice:			
Short Grain	1 C	2 C	60 minutes
Long Grain	1 C	1 1/2 C	50 minutes
Sweet	1 C	1 1/2 C	30 minutes

Basic Millet, Quinoa, or Amaranth
by Ivi Turner, San Diego, CA
(edited by Christine Dreher)

2 cups millet, quinoa or amaranth (soaked overnight)
4 cups of purified water
A few generous shakes of vegetable seasoning (see
      "Seasoning and Flavoring Foods" in the
      Introduction)

Millet:

See the beginning of this section for more information
about grains.

Drain the millet and place it in a skillet over medium heat
and toast lightly. When dry and lightly toasted, add the
water and vegetable seasoning. Bring to a boil, reduce heat
to low, and cover tightly. Cook about 20 minutes until the
water is gone. Serves 4 to 6.

Option: Add finely diced vegetables (onion, carrot,
zucchini, tomato, etc.) when you add the water. Cook as
directed above.

Amaranth and Quinoa:

Add the grains, water and seasoning to a medium-size
cooking pot and bring to a boil. Reduce heat, cover, and
simmer for 15 to 20 minutes until the water has
evaporated. Serves 4 to 6.

Option: Add one of the grain relish recipes in this chapter.

Black Bean and Corn Quinoa
by Sharna Gross, San Diego, CA

1 cup quinoa, cooked
1 cup black beans, cooked
1/4 cup fresh corn, cut off cob
1 Tbs. fresh basil, chopped
1 Tbs. fresh cilantro, chopped
1 tsp. cumin, ground
1 tsp. cayenne pepper
1 Tbs. extra virgin olive oil or flax seed oil
1 Tbs. lemon juice, freshly squeezed
Tomato Relish Salsa (see Sauces and Dips section)

See the beginning of this section for information about quinoa.

Toss all the ingredients together and let stand for 15 minutes to marinate. Place into individual bowls and garnish with a large spoonful of Tomato Relish Salsa. Makes 4 cups.

Black-Eyed Peas
with Mushrooms
Ivi Turner, San Diego, CA

1 3/4 cups fresh black-eyed peas, shelled, soaked, and
    sprouted
1/2 lb. mushrooms, sliced into 1/2 inch pieces
1 1/2 onions, peeled and diced
3 large tomatoes (vine ripened, low acid), chopped
3 Tbs. cilantro, minced
5 cups of purified water
4 Tbs. fresh tomato juice (vine-ripened, low-acid)
1 tsp. cumin seeds
1 inch cinnamon stick
4 cloves garlic, minced
2 tsp. ground coriander
1 tsp. ground cumin
1/2 tsp. turmeric
1/4 tsp. cayenne
2 tsp. vegetable seasoning, (see "Seasoning and
    Flavoring Foods" in the Introduction)
1/2 tsp. dulse, to taste

Add the whole cumin seeds and cinnamon stick to the
tomato juice over high heat. Let them sizzle for 5 seconds.
Add the onions and garlic. Stir fry until the onions begin
to brown on the edges. Add the mushrooms and stir fry
until they begin to wilt. Add the tomatoes, ground
coriander, ground cumin, turmeric, and cayenne. Stir and
cook for 1 minute. Cover, reduce to low heat, and let the
mixture simmer in its own juices for 10 minutes.

In a separate pot, cover the peas with water and bring to a
boil; simmer them until tender. Add the mushroom
mixture, dulse, vegetable seasoning, and cilantro to the
peas and water. Stir to mix and simmer, uncovered, on
medium-low heat for another 30 minutes, stirring
occasionally. Remove the cinnamon stick. Serves 4.

Cereal: Quinoa
Raisins
by Ivi Turner , San Diego, CA

1 cup quinoa
Handful of raisins
2 cups of purified water
Fresh or dried fruits (optional)

See the beginning of this section for more information about grains.

Boil the water. Add the quinoa and raisins. Stir, lower heat and cover. Cook approximately 15 to 20 minutes until the water has been absorbed.

Option: Chop and add assorted dried or fresh fruits such as apples, dates, or bananas. See the "Almond Milk" recipe in the Dessert section.

Amaranth may be substituted for quinoa (it has a lighter and more slippery texture). Serve with stevia, maple syrup, cinnamon, or honey.

Corny Quinoa
by Angela Green

2 cups quinoa, cooked
Hot red peppers, diced, to taste
1/4 cup celery, minced
Basil, dried, to taste
2 Tbs. lemon juice, freshly squeezed
1/2 cup corn kernels, cut off cob
1/2 cup bell peppers, chopped

See "About Corn" in the Vegetables section for more
information. Also, see the beginning of this section for
more information about quinoa.

Cook the quinoa with the diced hot red peppers, celery,
basil, and lemon juice. When the quinoa is done, add the
fresh corn kernels and the bell peppers. Mix with the
quinoa, cover, and remove from the heat. Let stand about
half an hour before serving.

Gourmet Grains
by Sherry Baquial, San Diego, CA

3 cups cooked grains, (brown rice, quinoa, or millet)
1/4 cup extra virgin olive oil flax seed oil
1 avocado, ripe, peeled, and de-seeded
1/2 red onion, peeled and chopped
1/2 cucumber, chopped
1/2 cup cilantro, chopped
Vegetable seasoning, to taste (see "Seasoning and
**   Flavoring Foods" in the Introduction)**

See the beginning of this section for more information about grains.

Add the oil to the almost-cool grains, adding extra oil to the grains if they still appear dry. Mash in the avocado. Then add the rest of the ingredients, slowly mixing in the vegetable seasoning last, to taste. Serves 6.

Maple Millet
with Sweet and Sour Carrots
by Sharna Gross, San Diego, CA

2 cups millet, cooked
1/2 onion, peeled and diced
3 carrots, diced into 1/4 inch cubes
1/4 cup maple syrup
4 Tbs. apple cider vinegar
1/2 cup vegetable stock (see the recipe in the Soups
section)

See the beginning of this section for more information
about millet.

Dry sauté the onions and carrots for about 3 minutes. Add
the maple syrup and vegetable stock and continue cooking
on medium-low heat for 3 to 5 minutes until the mixture
becomes slightly syrupy and the carrots are soft. Add the
vinegar and turn off the heat.

Toss the sweet and sour carrot mixture with the millet.
Makes 4 cups.

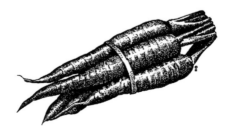

Middle Eastern Millet
by Ivi Turner, San Diego, CA

1 medium onion, peeled and chopped
1 medium red pepper, chopped
2 carrots
1 zucchini
1 1/8 cups vegetable broth (see the recipe in the Soups
        section)
1/4 cup raisins
1/4 cup golden raisins
3/8 tsp. cinnamon
1/8 tsp. turmeric
3/4 cup millet
1 Tbs. extra virgin olive oil or flax seed oil
Dulse and cayenne, to taste

In a non-stick large saucepan, over medium heat, dry
sauté the onion for about 5 minutes. Peel and cut the
carrots in half lengthwise and then cut them into 1/2-inch
pieces. Add the carrots and chopped red pepper to the
onions, lower heat, and cook covered for 5 minutes,
stirring occasionally.

Cut the zucchini in half lengthwise and then cut it into
1/2-inch pieces and add to the other vegetables. Continue
to cook for 5 more minutes, uncovered, stirring
occasionally.

Add the broth, raisins, cinnamon, turmeric, and millet.
Bring the vegetable mixture to a boil and cover. Lower
heat to simmer. Keep covered and simmer for 10 minutes.

Remove from the heat and let stand, covered, for 10 more
minutes. Transfer the mixture to a large bowl, fluffing
with a fork. Season with dulse and cayenne, then toss with
oil. Serve warm or at room temperature. Serves 4.

Pseudo-Southwestern Quinoa
by Angela Green, Boulder, CO

1 cup quinoa
1 tsp. ginger, minced
1 3/4 cups water
1/2 tsp. kelp powder or dulse
2 Tbs. lemon juice
3/4 tsp. cumin seeds
6 cayenne caps or 2 serrano or 2 fresno chili peppers
1 tsp. oregano, dried
1 avocado, diced and drenched with lime juice
4 green onions, peeled and chopped
1/4 cup extra virgin olive oil or flax seed oil
1 bunch cilantro, chopped

Crush the cumin seeds and boil them in 1/4 cup water with the ginger until half the water evaporates. Reduce the heat and add the remainder of the water.

Slit the peppers open lengthwise, cut out the seed cores, dice them, then add them to the water with the oregano, kelp powder, and lemon juice. Do not boil.

Rinse the quinoa thoroughly. Add it to the water and heat it until tiny bubbles appear. Immediately reduce heat to very low, cover, and cook for 20 to 25 minutes. When the quinoa cools, combine it with the oil, onions, avocado, and cilantro. Serves 2 to 4.

Relish for Grains:
Asparagus
by Sharna Gross, San Diego, CA

10 mushrooms, chopped
1 bunch asparagus, chopped
1 Tbs. red onion, peeled and finely chopped
1 Tbs. fresh basil, chopped
1 Tbs. vegetable seasoning (see :Seasoning and Flavoring
        Foods" in the Introduction)
1 Tbs. lemon juice, freshly squeezed
2 Tbs. extra virgin olive oil or flax seed oil
1 tsp. fresh rosemary, chopped

See "About Mushrooms" and "About Asparagus" in the
Vegetables section for more information.

Steam the mushrooms and asparagus until they are
slightly soft. While still hot, toss them with the remaining
ingredients and let the mixture stand for a few minutes so
the flavors can marry. Fold into 2 cups of grain.

Relish for Grains:
Asparagus and Thyme Salsa
by Sharna Gross, San Diego, CA

2 bunches asparagus, cut into 2-inch pieces
2 tomatoes (vine-ripened, low-acid), chopped
1/4 red onion, peeled and chopped
1 Tbs. fresh thyme, chopped
1 Tbs. fresh Italian parsley, chopped
2 Tbs. fresh corn, cut off cob
1 Tbs. apple cider vinegar
1 Tbs. lemon juice, freshly squeezed
2 Tbs. extra virgin olive oil or flax seed oil
1 Tbs. vegetable seasoning (see "Seasoning and
    Flavoring Foods" in the Introduction)

Preheat oven to 350°.

Place the asparagus in a roasting pan and add a little water for moisture. Roast in the oven until tender. Set aside.

Combine the remaining ingredients in a bowl to make the salsa relish. Pour the salsa over the warm asparagus. Toss and serve. Serves 4.

Serve mixed in your favorite cooked grain.

Relish for Grains:
Corn, Avocado, and Tomato
by Sharna Gross, San Diego, CA

3 Tbs. green onions, peeled and chopped
1/2 cup corn, cut off cob
1/2 cup tomatoes (vine-ripened, low-acid), chopped
1 Tbs. red onion, peeled and chopped fine
1 Tbs. fresh cilantro, chopped
1 Tbs. fresh basil, chopped
2 Tbs. vegetable seasoning (see "Seasoning and
    Flavoring Foods" in the Introduction)
3 Tbs. lemon juice, freshly squeezed
2 Tbs. extra virgin olive oil or flax seed oil
1 Tbs. dulse or other salt substitute (see "Seasoning and
    Flavoring Foods" in the Introduction)
1 avocado, diced

Mix all the ingredients, except the avocado, in a bowl. After allowing the mixture to stand for several minutes, lightly toss in the diced avocado. Fold the whole mixture into 4 cups of grain.

Relish for Grains:
Greek Salsa
by Sharna Gross, San Diego, CA

1 cup cucumber, chopped
1 cup tomato (vine-ripened, low-acid), chopped
1/2 cup red onion, peeled and chopped
3 Tbs. apple cider vinegar
3 Tbs. extra virgin olive oil or flax seed oil
3 Tbs. fresh oregano, chopped
3 Tbs. raw sprouted garbanzo beans, or cooked
      garbanzo beans, chopped coarsely

Combine the ingredients and then fold them into cold quinoa or other grain for a cool salad. Makes 2 1/2 cups.

Oregano

Relish for Grains:
Mango Avocado
by Sharna Gross, San Diego, CA

1 cup mango, chopped
1 cup avocado, chopped
1 cup red onion, peeled and chopped
3 Tbs. fresh basil, chopped
1 tsp. fresh mint, chopped
1 tsp. fresh cilantro, chopped
1 Tbs. lime juice, freshly squeezed
1 Tbs. lemon juice, freshly squeezed
Dash of cayenne pepper

Lightly fold the ingredients together and fold into a grain.
It is best when the grain is cold, as a cold grain salad.
Makes 2 1/2 cups.

Stuffed Acorn Squash
by Ivi Turner, San Diego, CA

2 acorn squash, cut in halves
2 small onions, peeled and minced
2 Tbs. extra virgin olive oil or flax seed oil
1/2 tsp. basil, dried
1/4 tsp. oregano, dried
1/8 tsp. sage, dried
2 cups millet, cooked
1/2 cup currants (similar to raisins)
Dulse, to taste (see "Seasoning and Flavoring Foods" in
    the Introduction)

Preheat oven to 375°.

See the beginning of this section for more information
about millet.

Bake the squash cut-side down in a baking dish with 1/2
inch of water until tender, about 30 to 45 minutes. Scoop
out the seeds. Let it cool.

In a medium-size non-stick saucepan, dry sauté the onions
for 5 to 6 minutes. Add the basil, oregano, and sage, and
cook for 2 minutes longer. Remove from the heat, add the
millet, currants, oil, and dulse, to taste. If the mixture
seems too dry, stir in a few drops of water or vegetable
broth. Let the millet mixture cool.

Fill the squash halves with the millet stuffing. Return the
squash to the oven, covered in foil, until heated. Or, to
serve later, wrap in foil, and store it in the refrigerator. To
re-heat, keep it wrapped in foil and heat it in a 350° oven
approximately 45 minutes or until heated through. Serves
2 to 4.

Vegan Millet-Crust Pizza
by Michael Goggins, Missoula, MT
edited by Christine Dreher

3 cups millet, cooked
1 bunch of fresh basil
1 1/2 cups carrots, shredded
1/2 bunch fresh spinach
1 cup shiitake mushrooms, diced
8 whole tomatoes (vine-ripened, low-acid)
1 cup broccoli, chopped
2 Tbs. basil, dried
1 Tbs. oregano, dried
1 cup green pepper, chopped
1 Tbs. garlic powder
1/2 cup green onion, peeled and diced
1/2 Tbs. cumin, ground
4 cloves garlic, minced and diced
1 Tbs. rosemary, dried

Preheat oven to 400°.

See the beginning of this section for more information about millet.

Begin by chopping 6 tomatoes and stew them with 1 1/2 cups of water. As the tomatoes cook down, add all of the dried spices and continue to stew for 15 to 20 minutes (add a little water if the consistency gets too thick).

While the tomatoes are stewing, use extra virgin olive oil to coat a wide, deep pan and spread the millet evenly in the pan. Toast in the oven for about 20 minutes or until slightly browned. Remove from the oven and spread the sauce over the crust. Freely sprinkle the basil and fresh vegetables, except the shredded carrots, over the pie. Cover with shredded carrots (or use "Vegan Rella" or tofu cheese if you are not cleansing) and the last 2 tomatoes sliced and arranged on top. Bake about 20 minutes or so until the pie is done in the middle. Serves 2 to 4.

Vegetable Chili
by Ivi Turner, San Diego, CA

1 small onion, peeled and chopped
1 cup zucchini, diced
1 cup yellow squash, diced
2 cups carrots, diced
10 large tomatoes (vine-ripened, low-acid), chopped
2 cups red kidney beans, soaked, sprouted, and cooked
3 Tbs. chili powder
1/2 tsp. basil, dried
1/2 tsp. oregano, dried
1/2 tsp. cumin, ground
2 large garlic cloves, peeled and minced
Juice of 1/2 lemon (optional; makes it tangy)
A few tsp. tomato juice (optional)

In a large non-stick pot, sauté the onion and garlic in a small amount of lemon juice or tomato juice until the onion is soft but not brown. Then mix the spices together and add them all at once to the onions.

Cook the mixture, stirring 30 seconds, and then add the zucchini, yellow squash, and carrots and blend well. Cook for 1 minute over low heat, stirring occasionally. Stir in the chopped tomatoes (with all the juices) and kidney beans. Bring to a boil. Reduce heat and simmer, partially covered, for 30 to 45 minutes until thickened. Partially remove the cover the last 15 minutes, if needed, to encourage thickening. Season with dulse and cayenne. Serves 4 to 6.

Option: Christine likes to pour the chili over cooked millet or quinoa for a healthy and hearty dish. You can also add some curry powder to this dish for an Indian flavor.

Dressings

Dressings

Avocado Dressing
by Ivi Turner, San Diego, CA

1 to 2 avocados
Dry mustard, to taste
Minced garlic, to taste
1 Tbs. apple cider vinegar
2 to 3 Tbs. extra virgin olive oil or flax seed oil
Natural vegetable seasoning, to taste (see "Seasoning and Flavoring Foods" in the Introduction)

Mash the ingredients (except the oil) together. Add the seasonings to taste. Add the oil to desired consistency. Use as a dip for vegetables or as a dressing on salad. Makes approximately 1 cup.

Carrot Juice Dressing/Sauce

by Jamey Dina, N.D. and Kim Sproul, N.D., Escondido, CA
From their cookbook <u>Un</u>cooking with Jamey & Kim

2 1/2 cups fresh carrot juice (depending on desired
thickness)
1 medium avocado
3 to 4 stalks celery
1/4 cup lemon juice, freshly squeezed

Mix all the ingredients in a blender until fully blended.
Add any other vegetable combination you like. For a less
sweet flavor, blend some cucumber into the recipe or add
more celery or other non-sweet vegetables. Cilantro gives
this recipe an excellent flavor. Or try fresh basil or red
pepper.

Carrot Juice Dressing/Sauce
(Indian Spice Version)

Carrot juice dressing/sauce (see above recipe)
Up to 1 1/2 tsp. turmeric
Up to 1/2 tsp. cumin
Up to 1/2 tsp. curry powder

Blend spices into the carrot juice dressing/sauce, to taste.

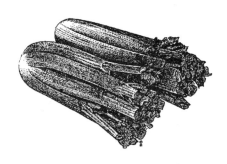

Citrus Vinaigrette Dressing
by Sharna Gross, San Diego, CA

3 Tbs. apple cider vinegar
1 cup extra virgin olive oil or flax seed oil
1 cup of citrus fruits (1/3 lemon, 1/3 lime, and 1/3 orange)
1 Tbs. zest from the citrus (grated peel)

Blend the ingredients, except the zest, in a blender to emulsify. Then add the zest. Use as a marinade for the "Layered Salad" in the Salads section, or as a vinaigrette dressing.

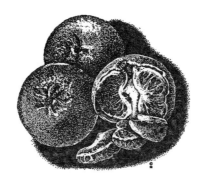

Creamy Lemon Herb Dressing
by Sharna Gross, San Diego, CA

1/2 cup extra virgin olive oil or flax seed oil
1/4 cup fresh lemon juice
1 tsp. lemon zest (grated peel)
1 tsp. orange zest (grated peel)
3 Tbs. assorted fresh herbs, chopped fine (thyme, basil,
    cilantro, or oregano)

Blend all the ingredients, except the herbs, until creamy
and smooth. Remove from the blender and add the herbs.
Serve over salad or vegetables. Makes one cup.

Fat Free Dressing/Sauce

by Jamey Dina, N.D. and Kim Sproul, N.D., Escondido, CA
From their cookbook <u>Un</u>cooking with Jamey & Kim

Tomatoes (vine-ripened, low-acid)
Carrots
**Lemons (use whole, peeled lemons or fresh-squeezed
      lemon juice)**
**Vegetable seasoning (optional; see "Seasoning and
      Flavoring Foods" in the Introduction)**

In a food processor or blender, blend the desired amounts
of all the ingredients, to taste. This is quick, easy, very
good-tasting and very good for you!

Add different spices or any other vegetables you like.
Celery, cucumber, lettuce, red pepper, cabbage and bok
choy all work well.

For a thicker dressing or sauce, use more carrots (or other
hard vegetables). For a thinner dressing or sauce, use more
tomato (or other watery vegetables). Pour over salad or
use as a dip or sauce.

Option: A little avocado may be added to "cream" up the
recipe, but then it will no longer be fat-free.

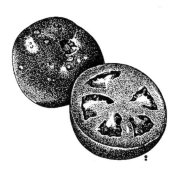

Garlic Dressing
by Laura Sellens, Missoula, MT

Juice of 4 lemons
1/4 cup of extra virgin olive oil or flax seed oil
1 1/2 tsp. cumin
1/4 cup of apple cider vinegar
3 garlic cloves, peeled and pressed

Mix all the ingredients well. Allow the garlic to stand in the liquid for a while before using.

Garlic Herb Salad Dressing
by Angela Green, Boulder, CO

Juice from one lemon
2 oz. flax seed oil
12 oz. extra virgin olive oil
Cayenne, to taste
2 tsp. dehydrated onion
3 large garlic cloves, pressed
1 Tbs. dried marjoram, crushed
2 Tbs. dried basil, crushed
1 tsp. dried savory, crushed
1 Tbs. dried green oregano, crushed
1 Tbs. vegetable broth mixed with 1 tsp. of vegetable
seasoning (optional; see broth recipe in the Soups
section and "Seasoning and Flavoring Foods" in
the Introduction)

Mix all the ingredients in a shaker bottle. Keep
refrigerated if you use flax seed oil.

Lime Cilantro Dressing
by Sharna Gross, San Diego, CA

1/4 cup extra virgin olive oil or flax seed oil
5 Tbs. apple cider vinegar
Juice of 5 limes, freshly squeezed
3 Tbs. fresh cilantro
1 Tbs. vegetable seasoning, (see "Seasoning and
      Flavoring Foods" in the Introduction)
1/2 tsp. cumin
1/2 tsp. cayenne pepper

Puree all the ingredients in a blender until smooth. Serve over salad. Makes 1 cup.

Pesto Dressing
by Ivi Turner, San Diego, CA

2 bunches fresh basil
1/4 to 1/2 bunch fresh parsley
4 to 6 garlic cloves, peeled and coarsely chopped
Juice of 1 lemon
1 Tbs. honey or maple syrup (or stevia to taste)
Extra virgin olive oil or flax seed oil, to taste

Place all the ingredients, except the oil, in a blender. Puree on high for 10 seconds. With the blender going, add the oil in a thin stream until desired consistency is reached.

Place the dressing in a tightly covered container and refrigerate. This dressing may be kept thick for dipping raw or lightly steamed vegetables or thinned and served as a dressing on salad or grains. Makes approximately 1 1/2 cups.

Parsley

Roasted Shallot and Red Pepper Dressing
by Sharna Gross, San Diego, CA

10 shallots, peeled and cut in half
4 red bell peppers, chopped
1 garlic clove
1 Tbs. vegetable seasoning (see "Seasoning and
 Flavoring Foods" in the Introduction)
1/4 cup apple juice, freshly squeezed
1 Tbs. apple cider vinegar
2 Tbs. lemon juice, freshly squeezed
4 Tbs. extra virgin olive oil or flax seed oil

Preheat Oven to 350°.

Place the shallots and red peppers in a roasting pan and roast in the oven until soft.

In a blender, puree all the ingredients together until smooth. Serve over salad or marinate vegetables with this fabulous dressing! Makes 2 cups.

Roasted Tomato and Basil Dressing
by Sharna Gross, San Diego, CA

6 to 8 Roma tomatoes or 3 to 4 regular tomatoes (vine-
    ripened, low-acid)
1/4 cup extra virgin olive oil or flax seed oil
3 Tbs. fresh lemon juice
1 Tbs. apple cider vinegar
1/4 cup vegetable juice, freshly squeezed
1 Tbs. vegetable seasoning (see "Seasoning and
    Flavoring Foods" in the Introduction)
1 bunch fresh basil, coarsely chopped

Heat a cast iron skillet until hot and place the tomatoes in
the pan. Char the outside of the tomatoes until soft and
brown.

Puree all the ingredients in a blender, including the
tomatoes, until soft. Reserve the vegetable juice for last,
adding slowly to control the consistency so that it is not
too thin. Store covered in the refrigerator. Makes 1 cup.

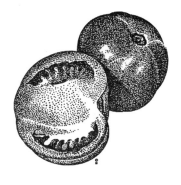

Sundried Tomato and Herb Dressing
by Ivi Turner, San Diego, CA

6 to 8 sundried tomatoes, sliced
6 large basil leaves
1 tsp. fresh tarragon
1/4 tsp. oregano, dried
1/4 tsp. mustard, dried
1/4 cup apple cider vinegar
3/4 cup flax seed oil or extra virgin olive oil

Put everything except the oil in a blender. Puree on high speed for 15 seconds. With the blender going, add the oil in a thin stream until emulsified. Pour into a covered container, close tightly, and keep refrigerated. Makes approximately 1 1/2 cups.

Variations of Vinaigrette Dressing
by Sharna Gross, San Diego, CA

1/4 cup apple cider vinegar
3 Tbs. lemon juice, freshly squeezed
1/2 cup extra virgin olive oil or flax seed oil

Blend all the ingredients and serve. Makes 3/4 cup.

Options:

- Substitute lime or orange juice for lemon juice

- Add 2 Tbs. of stevia or maple syrup and 1 tsp. of cayenne for sweet and sour dressing.

- Add 1/4 cup of pureed raspberries and 3 Tbs. of maple syrup for a raspberry vinaigrette.

Add 1/4 cup of pureed mango and up to 1 jalapeño pepper for a spicy, sweet, mango dressing.

You can add pureed fruit of any kind to make different dressings. For marinades, alternate fresh herbs or spices and toss either raw vegetables or cooked vegetables in the vinaigrette.

Dressings

Sauces and Dips

Sauces and Dips

Broccomole

by Dan Napier, Greentree Chef, San Diego, CA

1 1/2 cups broccoli stems, well-cooked
1 1/2 Tbs. lemon juice, freshly squeezed
1/4 tsp. cumin or 1/2 tsp. vegetable seasoning mix (see
    "Seasoning and Flavoring Foods" in the
    Introduction)
1/4 tsp. garlic powder
1/2 tomato, (vine-ripened, low-acid), diced
1 green onion, peeled and chopped
1 green chili pepper, chopped

Cut off the outside tough skin of the broccoli stems. Place
the broccoli stems, lemon juice, cumin, and garlic powder
in a blender or food processor and puree until smooth.

Christine prefers to blend the tops of the green onions and
the green chili pepper with the broccoli in the food
processor for a smooth consistency and greener color. Save
the white part of the chopped green onions to add with
the remaining ingredients.

Transfer to a bowl. Add the remaining ingredients and
mix well. For best flavor, chill before serving. Makes 2
cups or 8 servings.

Option: If you like it spicy, Christine recommends
blending a jalapeño pepper (whole, with seeds) with the
broccoli or cayenne pepper, to taste.

Per serving: 14 calories, 1g protein, 0.1g fat, 3 g
carbohydrates, 0 cholesterol, 5 mg. sodium. This is a fat
free version of Guacamole. (Avocados have approximately
30 g of fat each.) So if you are trying to loose weight eat
broccomole and if you are trying to gain weight, eat
guacamole.

Garlic Lemon Dip or Spread
by Angela Green

1/2 cup of lemon juice, freshly squeezed
2 large heads of garlic
1/2 cup extra virgin olive oil or flax seed oil

Peel and crush the garlic. Combine with the liquids. If it is
too watery, add more garlic. Keeps about one month
refrigerated. Tastes great on artichokes, see the Vegetables
section.

Eggplant Dip
with Cilantro, Cumin, and Red Peppers
by Sharna Gross, San Diego, CA

1 large eggplant
2 large red bell peppers
1 head garlic
2 Tbs. cilantro, chopped
1 tsp. cumin
3 Tbs. extra virgin olive oil or flax seed oil
3 Tbs. lemon juice, freshly squeezed
1 Tbs. fresh garlic, pressed

Preheat oven 350°.

See "About Eggplant" in the Vegetables section for information.

Roast the eggplant, the bell peppers, and the head of garlic in the oven until soft. When cooled, press the garlic out of the bulb and puree all the ingredients in the blender until the desired consistency is achieved. This makes an excellent dip for fresh vegetables. Makes 3 cups.

Guacamole
by Christine Dreher, San Diego, CA

3 Haas avocados (ripe)
1/2 cup red onion, peeled and minced
1 garlic clove, pressed
1 Tbs. lemon juice, freshly squeezed
Cayenne, to taste
Fresh cilantro, for garnish

Cut the avocados in half, remove the seed, and scoop out into a bowl. Add 1 Tbs. of fresh lemon juice and mash with a fork until smooth. Add the onion and garlic. Add a pinch of cayenne or more to spice it up. Serve with a few sprigs of fresh cilantro on top.

Guacamole de la Fresca
by Christine Dreher, San Diego, CA

Same recipe as above, but add one cup of salsa fresca (see the recipe in this section) and stir. Good as a south of the border dressing for salads or as a dip.

Hummus
by Sharna Gross, San Diego, CA

2 cups sprouted, raw (or cooked) garbanzo beans
5 Tbs. vegetable seasoning (see "Seasoning and
        Flavoring Foods" in the Introduction)
3 garlic cloves, peeled and chopped
1 Tbs. fresh Italian parsley, chopped
4 Tbs. lemon juice, freshly squeezed
1/4 cup extra virgin olive oil or flax seed oil
1/2 cup sunflower seeds, sprouted

Puree all the ingredients until soft and smooth. Serve with
your favorite raw vegetables. Makes 3 cups.

Lime Avocado Sauce
with Cumin and Cilantro
by Sharna Gross, San Diego, CA

4 ripe avocados
4 Tbs. lime juice, freshly squeezed
1/4 cup extra virgin olive oil or flax seed oil
1 Tbs. cumin
3 Tbs. fresh cilantro, chopped
2 Tbs. vegetable seasoning, (see "Seasoning and
     Flavoring Foods" in the Introduction)
3 Tbs. red onions, peeled and chopped
1 garlic clove, chopped

Puree all the ingredients in a blender until smooth. Serve over vegetables or grain dishes. Makes 4 cups.

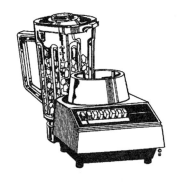

Marinated Herb and Garlic Artichoke Dip
by Sharna Gross, San Diego, CA

4 large artichokes
2 cups lemon herb vinaigrette (see Dressings section)
2 Tbs. fresh Italian parsley, chopped
1 Tbs. garlic, peeled and chopped
1/4 cup garbanzo beans, raw and sprouted, or cooked
1/4 cup vegetable broth (see Soups section)

See "About Artichokes" in the Vegetables section for more information.

Boil the artichokes in a large pot of water until soft and the center is easily pulled out. Pull the outer leaves off the artichoke so only the soft leaves and bottoms remain.

In a food processor, pulse the artichoke with the remaining ingredients, except the vegetable stock, until thick or coarse. Add the stock to desired consistency.

Note: Do not add too much broth if you desire a thick consistency. Makes about 4 cups.

Mock Gravy (Raw)
by Jamey Dina, N.D. and Kim Sproul, N.D., Escondido, CA
From their cookbook *Uncooking with Jamey & Kim*

1 3/4 cups sprouted sunflower seeds (measured after
 sprouting)
1/2 cup purified water or cucumber juice
1/2 to 1 medium tomato (vine-ripened, low-acid)
1/2 to 1 stalk celery
1/2 medium avocado
1 to 2 garlic cloves, peeled
2 Tbs. lemon juice, freshly squeezed
2 1/2 Tbs. Vegetable Power seasoning (see "Seasoning
 and Flavoring Foods" in the Introduction)

In a blender, blend all the ingredients except the avocado
and seasoning to a creamy consistency. Then add the
avocado and seasoning; mix until blended. For a thinner
gravy, add the whole tomato or more water or juice. For a
thicker gravy, add less water or juice or more sunflower
seeds.

Pesto
by Jessie Ann, Chino Valley, AZ

Finely chop the following in proportions to your taste:

Fresh basil (lots, or at least one bunch)
Garlic
Parsley
Sprouted sunflower seeds
Touch of vegetable seasoning, (see "Seasoning and
**   Flavoring Foods" in the Introduction)**
Extra virgin olive oil or flax seed oil
Nutritional yeast for cheese-like flavor

Christine recommends blending all the ingredients in the blender, except the oil. After blending, add the oil a little at a time until desired consistency is created.

Roasted Garlic Spread
by Ivi Turner, San Diego, CA

1 large head of garlic
Juice of 1/2 lemon
Millet rice cakes, (available at health food stores)
Extra virgin olive oil or flax seed oil, brushed on garlic
during or after cooking (optional)

Preheat oven to 375°.

Cut the top off the garlic and place the root side down in roasting pan. Sprinkle with lemon juice and cover. Roast at 375° until soft, approximately 60 to 90 minutes. Slice the top off so that the melted cloves can be scooped out and spread on vegetables or millet rice cakes. Serves 1 to 2.

Option: Use the millet crust from the "Vegan Millet-Crust Pizza" in the Grains section if you cannot locate millet rice cakes.

Roasted Vegetable Sauce
by Sharna Gross, San Diego, CA

1 cup carrots, chopped
1 cup red onions, peeled and chopped
1 cup broccoli, chopped
1 cup mushrooms, chopped
1 cup red bell peppers, chopped
2 Tbs. vegetable seasoning (see "Seasoning and
        Flavoring Foods" in the Introduction)
2 Tbs. lemon juice, freshly squeezed
3 Tbs. extra virgin olive oil or flax seed oil
1 Tbs. dulse or other salt substitute

Preheat oven to 350°.

Place all the chopped vegetables in a roasting pan and
roast in the oven, tossing occasionally, until light brown
and soft. Puree all the ingredients coarsely in a blender
until sauce consistency is achieved. Makes 6 cups.

Salsa Fresca
by Christine Dreher, San Diego, CA

10 to 12 Roma tomatoes (vine-ripened, low-acid)
1 cup red onion, peeled and minced
1 jalapeño pepper
1/2 cup green chilies, minced
1/2 cup fresh cilantro, finely minced
2 cloves of garlic, peeled and crushed
1 1/2 Tbs. lemon juice, freshly squeezed
Cayenne, to taste

Dice the tomatoes into small pieces and place into a medium-size bowl. Remove the seeds from the jalapeño and mince it into small pieces; also mince the green chilies.

Add the chilies, jalapeño, onions, cilantro, garlic, and lemon juice to the bowl and mix thoroughly. Add cayenne, to taste. Serves 4.

Option: For a sweeter salsa, add 1/2 cup of grated carrots. Also, all the ingredients can be briefly blended for a smoother texture.

Salsa Verde
by Sharna Gross, San Diego, CA

1 cup fresh parsley
1 cup fresh basil
1 cup fresh mint
1 cup fresh cilantro
1 bunch green onions
1/2 to 1 cup extra virgin olive oil or flax seed oil
4 Tbs. lemon juice, freshly squeezed
3 Tbs. vegetable seasoning, (see "Seasoning and
        Flavoring Foods" in the Introduction)
1 Tbs. dulse or other salt substitute
2 cloves garlic, peeled and coarsely chopped
4 Tbs. apple cider vinegar

Puree all the ingredients in a blender until smooth and
completely blended. Makes 4 cups.

Smoked Tomato
with Basil Sauce
by Sharna Gross, San Diego, CA

6 Roma tomatoes (vine-ripened, low-acid)
1 bunch fresh basil
1 Tbs. vegetable seasoning, (see "Seasoning and
       Flavoring Foods" in the Introduction)
13 Tbs. extra virgin olive oil or flax seed oil

Preheat oven to 450°.

Place a cast iron skillet into the preheated oven and heat until very hot. Place the tomatoes in the skillet and cook until the tomatoes are smoking. Turn off the oven and let them set for about 20 minutes until soft. Remove them from the oven and puree them immediately in a blender with the other ingredients.

Spaghetti Sauce (Raw Tomato Sauce)

by Jamey Dina, N.D. and Kim Sproul, N.D., Escondido, CA
From their cookbook <u>Un</u>cooking with Jamey & Kim

Fresh tomatoes (vine-ripened, low-acid)
Tomato Power or dried tomatoes (see "Seasoning and
    Flavoring Foods" in the Introduction)
Italian seasonings (health store pre-mixed or blend your
    own)

Puree the tomatoes in a blender or food processor. Add
desired quantities of the other ingredients to taste. The
Tomato Power or dried tomatoes will make the sauce
thicker, darker and more like traditional tomato sauce.
Pour over "Mock Spaghetti" (see the Vegetables section).

Note: We suggest drying them yourself, because dried
tomatoes in the stores have usually been heated and are
therefore more acidic.

Spaghetti Sauce (Raw)
"I can't believe it's not Butter Sauce"
by Jamey Dina, N.D. and Kim Sproul, N.D., Escondido, CA
From their cookbook <u>Uncooking</u> *with Jamey & Kim*

Flax seed oil (we recommend up to 2 Tbs. per person)
Fresh garlic, to taste
Any summer squash (optional)

See "About Squash - Summer Varieties" in the Vegetables section for more information.

Blend the flax seed oil (do not heat) with garlic and optional squash (for creaminess). Pour over "Mock Spaghetti" (see the Vegetables section) like butter sauce. If desired, add other seasonings (see "Seasoning and Flavoring Foods" in the Introduction).

Sunflower-Lentil Dip

by Jamey Dina, N.D. and Kim Sproul, N.D., Escondido, CA
From their cookbook *Uncooking with Jamey & Kim*

1 1/2 cups sunflower seeds, sprouted (measured after
    sprouting)
1 cup lentils, sprouted
4 medium carrots, well-chopped
3 to 4 stalks celery, well-chopped
1/3 cup lemon juice, freshly squeezed
3 cloves garlic, peeled and coarsely chopped
2 Tbs. each of Vegetable Power and Tomato Power or
    other vegetable seasoning (optional, but
    recommended, see "Seasoning and Flavoring
    Foods" in the Introduction)

Blend all the ingredients in a food processor until very
well-mixed. Great served with carrots or celery sticks, or
as a filling for nori rolls (see the Vegetables section),
lettuce, cabbage, chard, etc.

Tomato Relish Salsa
by Sharna Gross, San Diego, CA

2 large tomatoes (vine-ripened, low-acid), diced
1/2 red onion, peeled and diced
1 Tbs. extra virgin olive oil or flax seed oil
1 Tbs. lemon juice, freshly squeezed
1 Tbs. fresh cilantro, chopped
1 roasted chili, finely chopped
1 roasted red pepper, finely chopped

Toss all the ingredients together; let stand at least 1/2 hour to marinade, then serve. Makes 3 cups.

Vinegar Onion Sauce
with Herbs
by Sharna Gross, San Diego, CA

4 red onions, peeled and cut in quarters
1 garlic clove, peeled
1/2 cup apple cider vinegar
1/4 cup extra virgin olive oil or flax seed oil
3 Tbs. vegetable seasoning, (see "Seasoning and
**   Flavoring Foods" in the Introduction)**
1 Tbs. fresh thyme, chopped
1 Tbs. fresh sage, chopped
1 Tbs. fresh oregano, chopped

Preheat oven to 300°.

Place all the ingredients in a baking pan. Mix and cover with foil. Bake in the oven until the onions are soft.

Remove from the oven and let stand for 3 hours. Then either puree as a sauce or eat as a vegetable. Makes 4 cups, pureed.

The Cleanse Cookbook   **197**

Sauces and Dips

Desserts

Desserts

Almond Milk Recipe
by Molly Weiler, Boulder, CO

1 cup almonds (soaked overnight)
4 cups purified water
Maple syrup or Stevia to taste
1 cinnamon stick

Liquefy the almonds and water in a blender or a Vita Mix.
Strain the mixture through a cheesecloth. Add sweetener
to taste and plop in cinnamon stick. Cover and store in the
refrigerator. Will stay fresh in refrigerator for a few days.

Notes from Molly: I used Stevia instead of maple syrup
and I put in a cinnamon stick instead of ground cinnamon
because I don't like the dry chalky effect it can have. I
think it's great. I was really surprised at how much the
flavor resembled soy milk (a thinner consistency though).

Smoothies made with almond milk can include frozen
bananas, fresh fruit, maple syrup, super green powder,
flax oil, etc. It's easy to improvise. It's also great plain in a
glass. I think it's my new favorite milk substitute!

Apple Delight
by Emily Mudhar Fung, Blackheath, London England

2 kiwis
2 bananas
2 fresh dates
2 apples

Blend the above fruits together, except for the apples, until smooth. Chop the apples and pour the blended mixture over the apples and serve immediately. Serves 1 to 2.

Option: Christine likes to sprinkle a little ground cinnamon on top.

Baked Apples
by Sharna Gross, San Diego, CA

4 apples, cored and cut in half
6 cups fresh apple juice
1/4 cup maple syrup (or stevia to taste)

Preheat Oven to 325°

Place the apples, cut side down, in a baking dish and pour the juice and sweetener over the apples.

Cover with foil and bake until apples are soft but not mushy. Let cool and serve in juice. Yummy! Serves 4.

Option: Christine suggests adding 1 tsp. of ground cinnamon to the juice.

Banana Pudding
by Jamey Dina, N.D. and Kim Sproul, N.D., Escondido, CA
From their cookbook <u>Un</u>cooking with Jamey & Kim

Bananas (bananas are speckled when truly ripe)
Apple, papaya, or any other fruit (optional)

Slice bananas (and other optional fruit) and mix together
in a food processor or blender. Keep adding the fruit until
you have the desired quantity. Chill if desired.

Carob Banana Pudding

Bananas
Raw carob powder, to taste
1 apple, sliced (optional)

Blend all ingredients in a food processor or blender until
you have the desired quantity and flavor. Chill if desired.

Berry Pudding

Bananas
Fresh or frozen berries of choice

Mix the bananas and berries together in a food processor
or blender. Keep adding the fruit until you have the
desired quantity. For a more "berry" flavor, add more
berries; for less berry flavor, add fewer berries.
Strawberries or blueberries are very good in this recipe.
No need to chill if you are using frozen berries.

Candied Carrots and Apples
by Christine Dreher, San Diego, CA

2 to 3 green or red apples, cored and coarsely chopped
1 lb. carrots, sliced diagonally into bite-size pieces
1 Tbs. maple syrup (or stevia to taste)
1 tsp. cinnamon
1 tsp. extra virgin olive oil or flax seed oil (optional)
1/2 cup fresh apple juice
Dash of nutmeg

Steam the carrots in a steamer until almost tender.

While the carrots are steaming, cook the stevia or maple syrup, apple juice, cinnamon, nutmeg and apples over a low heat, stirring often, until the sauce starts to thicken and the apples become tender.

Add the carrots to the saucepan and mix with the other ingredients. Continue to simmer and stir two more minutes. Turn off the heat and add the optional oil. Serve hot as a delicious treat! Makes 4 servings.

Fruit Shake #1

by Jamey Dina, N.D. and Kim Sproul, N.D., Escondido, CA
From their cookbook <u>Uncooking</u> *with Jamey & Kim*

**3/4 cup fresh apple juice (make your own, or buy it in
    the refrigerated section of a health food store;
    un-refrigerated juices were heated and are acidic)**
3 to 5 bananas, depending on desired thickness
Fresh or frozen berries, to taste

Blend all the ingredients thoroughly in a blender. Bananas
may be frozen first (peel before freezing) for a more
milkshake-like consistency.

Fruit Shake #2

**3/4 cup fresh apple juice (make your own, or buy it in
    the refrigerated section of a health food store;
    un-refrigerated juices were heated and are acidic)**
**1 orange, freshly juiced (be sure it is ripe; unripe citrus is
    acidic in metabolic reactions)**
2 to 3 fresh or frozen bananas (peel before freezing)

Pour the apple juice and orange juice into a blender; then
add enough bananas to make 2 cups worth of liquid (most
blenders have measuring lines on the side). Blend
thoroughly.

Fruit Shake #3

In a base of freshly made fruit juice, blend together your
own unique combination of fresh berries, peaches,
nectarines, mangos, papaya, pineapple, grapes, etc. Be
creative and have fun!

Ginger Rice Pudding
by Sharna Gross, San Diego, CA

2 cups grains (brown rice, millet, or quinoa)
4 cups fresh apple juice
1 Tbs. fresh chopped ginger
1/2 cup maple syrup (or stevia to taste)

See the beginning of the Grains section for more information about cooking grains.

Cook the grain until soft, using the apple juice instead of water. The grain will be a liquid consistency when done. Add the ginger and stevia or maple syrup and cook an additional 10 minutes until creamy.

Can be eaten warm or layered in a glass dish or non-stick dish to cool. Cut into squares and serve. Serves 6 to 8.

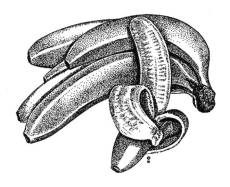

Desserts

Juice Slushes
by Jamey Dina, N.D. and Kim Sproul, N.D., Escondido, CA
From their cookbook <u>Un</u>cooking with Jamey & Kim

Any vegetable or fruit juice combination of your choice, such as carrot, celery, beet, cucumber, apple, kale, collard greens, spinach, Jerusalem artichoke, burdock root, jicama, etc.

Make your choice of juice and freeze it in containers with mouths at least as wide as any other part of the container. If the mouth of the container is smaller than the rest of the container, you will not be able to get the frozen juice out of it until it is mostly thawed and that will not work for this recipe. Close the lids before putting the containers in the freezer.

There are two methods to making juice slushes.

Food Processing Method:

Remove a frozen juice container from the freezer. Keep the lid on and place it in very warm water only long enough to be able to break it up into several pieces with a knife or other tool. When broken into several pieces, pour into a food processor and mix until desired consistency is achieved. Eat with a spoon.

For extra flavor and super-nutrition, add one of the suggested nourishing powders listed in the method below.

Manual Method:

Remove a frozen juice container from the freezer and place it in very warm water for several minutes or until you have one large "ice cube" of juice floating in the just-melted juice. The lid should be kept on during this process. Then open the lid and pour the contents into a large bowl, preferably one with high sides. With a knife, break apart the large cube into several pieces and crush further with a manual potato masher (or anything that will crush well). With a little patience, you can achieve the consistency of a "slurpy" or "slush." Eat with a spoon.

For extra nutrition and taste, you can add a super green food mix, wheat grass juice powder, algae, spirulina, chlorella, etc. If adding any of these, do so just before you are ready to eat; not before freezing. Completely dried powders will not be adversely affected by freezing, but if they get wet, they will lose some of their vital life force if left sitting around or frozen. Eat for breakfast, lunch, dinner, or snacks.

Note: If the consistency becomes too watery, add some crushed ice and re-blend.

Mango Sorbet
with Strawberry Compote
by Sharna Gross, San Diego, CA

4 mangos, peeled, cut, and pureed
1 1/2 cups fresh apple juice
1 cup strawberries, cleaned and trimmed

Mix the mango puree with 1 cup of apple juice. Freeze in ice cube trays.

Remove the cubes and pulse then in a food processor until they reach sorbet consistency. If too watery, freeze again and then puree again. Cook the strawberries with the remaining apple juice until the strawberries are soft and falling apart. Cool and serve with the sorbet.

Maple Millet Cakes
with 3 Topping Variations
by Sharna Gross, San Diego, CA

2 cups cooked millet
1/4 cup maple syrup

See the beginning of the Grains section for more information about cooking millet.

Toss the millet while warm and place in a glass baking dish. Cool. Cut millet into disk-shape cakes.

Option: If you prefer not to use maple syrup, use 1/2 cup of fresh squeezed apple juice cooked down to 1/4 cup and add a little stevia for sweetness.

Pour 3 tsp. of maple syrup over the millet cakes and garnish with a fruit topping. You can use blueberries, strawberries, boysenberries, or raspberries. See the "Poached Pears with Blueberry Maple Sauce" recipe in this section for the fruit topping instructions. Makes 6 cakes.

Mock Yogurt
by Jamey Dina, N.D. and Kim Sproul, N.D., Escondido, CA
From their cookbook _Uncooking with Jamey & Kim_

Papaya puree
Fresh or frozen berries of choice (blueberries are good)
Bananas (optional for a thicker yogurt)
Fresh apple juice (optional for a thinner yogurt)
Any other fruit desired (optional)

Papaya puree is the main ingredient in this recipe. You can find this pre-made in the refrigerated section of some health food stores (raw juices are _always_ refrigerated), or make your own.

Pour the papaya puree into a blender, add the other ingredients to taste and blend until creamy. Pour into a cup or bowl and eat with a spoon like yogurt.

Poached Pears
with Blueberry Sauce
by Sharna Gross, San Diego, CA

4 pears, peeled
4 cups purified water
4 cups fresh apple juice
1 cup blueberries
1/4 cup maple syrup (or stevia to taste)
1 tsp. lemon juice, freshly squeezed

In a cooking pot, stand the whole pears side by side and pour the apple juice over the pears until the tops of the pears are covered. Cover and poach over medium heat until soft. Remove from heat. Let them cool in the juice in a serving container.

Puree 1/2 cup of blueberries with the stevia or maple syrup and lemon juice. Add 1/2 cup of fresh whole blueberries. Let sit for a half hour. When the pears have cooled, cover each pear with 1/4 of the sauce. Serves 4.

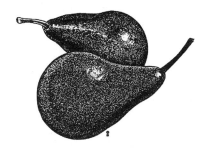

Raw Fruit Pie
by Ivi Turner, San Diego, CA

2 cups figs
10 apples, shredded (leave skin on)
1 cup dates (non-sulfured)
Fruit for pureed topping (see below)
Strawberries or coconut, for garnish

Prepare the millet crust (see below). Blend the figs and dates in a food processor. Then spread them on the crust. Top with shredded apples.

Choose your pureed topping: blueberries, kiwi, papaya, or persimmons. This will be your third layer. Last, garnish with cut strawberries, coconut, etc. Serves 6 to 8.

Millet Crust

3 cups puffed millet (available in health food stores)
1 cup dates
1 cup raisins
1/2 tsp. cinnamon

Mix together all the ingredients until sticky and blended. Shape into a pie crust in a pie pan and refrigerate. Proceed with the recipe for the Raw Fruit Pie.

Summer Fruit Salad
by Ivi Turner, San Diego, CA

1 banana, cut in thin diagonals
1 cup strawberries, sliced
3 ripe peaches, peeled and sliced
2 kiwi, peeled and sliced
1 cup red seedless grapes, halved
1/3 cup coconut, shredded
1/2 tsp. cinnamon
1/2 tsp. nutmeg
Juice of 1 lemon mixed with water to make 1/4 cup
Butter lettuce leaves, (to be eaten with the fruit)
1 cup cherries, pitted

Combine the fruits and the coconut in a bowl, reserving the cherries. Toss gently with the lemon juice. Arrange lettuce leaves on plates. Spoon salad into leaves, sprinkle with cinnamon, nutmeg, and cherries. Serves 2 to 4.

Sweet Potato Pudding
by Christine Dreher, San Diego, CA

2 large sweet potatoes
1/2 tsp. cinnamon
Fresh apple juice, to sweeten to taste

Preheat oven to 400°.

Poke holes in the cleaned sweet potatoes and wrap them in foil. Bake for 45 to 60 minutes, depending on size, until the potatoes are soft.

Cool the potatoes in the refrigerator for 30 minutes or more. Blend the sweet potatoes and cinnamon thoroughly in a blender until smooth. Add a little apple juice for sweetness. Chill and serve. Serves 2.

Velvety Applesauce
by Jessica Frank, Hudson, FL

1 bag cortland apples, cored and de-seeded
1 Tbs. cinnamon
1/4 tsp. cloves
1/4 tsp. nutmeg
1/4 tsp. allspice
Stevia, raw honey, or maple syrup, to taste

Blend the apples in a food processor on high until there are no more lumps. You may need to add some water. Place the apples in a bowl and add the spices and stevia, honey, or maple syrup to taste. Delicious!

Desserts

The Cleanse Cookbook

Resources and References

Resources and References

The Cleanse Cookbook

Candida Information
H.S.O. Information Packet

> Christine's Cleanse Corner
> Christine Dreher
> P.O. Box 421423
> San Diego, CA 92142
> Info: 858-673-0224
> Orders Toll Free: 1-877-673-0224
> www.TransformYourHealth.com
> or www.TransformYourLife.com
> Email: seechristine@earthlink.net

Yeast Control In Seven Days, Yeast Free Cookbook, The Digestion Digest Manual

> Sal D'Onofrio, D.N., D.D.
> 409 N. Pacific Coast Hwy #275
> Redondo Beach, CA 90277
> 1-888-231-0738
> www.HealthGuardians.com
> Email: Natdr@aol.com

Cleanse Information and Products
Cleanse & Purify Thyself books, *The Arise & Shine Cleanse Program Guide,* Cleanse Products and pH papers. Available from your local Arise & Shine Cleanse Distributor or:

> Christine's Cleanse Corner
> Christine Dreher
> P.O. Box 421423
> San Diego, CA 92142
> Info: 858-673-0224
> Orders Toll Free: 1-877-673-0224
> www.TransformYourHealth.com
> or www.TransformYourLife.com
> Email: seechristine@earthlink.net

Resources and References

Fighting Radiation and Chemical Pollutants with Foods, Herbs and Vitamins
> Steven R. Schecter, N.D.
> Vitality Ink
> P.O. Box 294
> Encinitas, CA 92024
> (or contact Christine)

Tissue Cleansing Through Bowel Management, Dr. Patient Handbook, Benard Jensen's Vegetable Seasoning
> Bernard Jensen, Int'l.
> 1914 W. Mission Rd. #F
> Escondido, CA 92029
> 760-291-1255

Raw Food Cookbooks

Living in the Raw
> Cookbook by Rose Lee Calabro
> P.O. Box 2274
> Santa Cruz, CA 95063
> 1-877-557-4711

The Garden of Eden Raw Fruit & Vegetable Recipes
> Phyllis Avery
> Hygeia Enterprises
> P.O. Box 3693
> Vista, CA 92085-3693
> Info: 760-630-8288
> Orders Toll Free: 1-877-246-3885

Uncooking with Jamey & Kim
> Jamey Dina, N.D., and Kim Sproul, N.D.
> HealthForce Nutritionals
> 1835A. S. Centre City Pkwy. #411
> Escondido, CA 92025-6504
> Info: 760-747-8822
> Order: 1-800-357-2717

Grains

Quinoa
> Available in health food stores or contact:
> Allergy Resources, Inc.
> 2647 Brookridge
> Palmer Lake, CO 80133
> 1-800-USE-FLAX

Organic Foods

Farming in Nature's Image - An Ecological Approach to Agriculture, by Piper and Soule.

"A Celebration of Growing Food Around the World," from *The Good Earth,* by Michael Ableman.

Organically Grown Food: A Consumer's Guide, by Theodore Wood Carlat.

Meeting the Expectations of the Land, by Jackson, Berry and Coleman, editors.

Naturopathic Physicians

> American Association of Naturopathic Physicians
> 2366 E. Lake Ave. E, Suite 322
> Seattle, WA 98102
> Fax 206-323-7610
> Send $5 for a directory of their U.S. members

> American Holistic Medical Association
> 4101 Lake Boone Trail, Suite 201
> Raleigh, NC 27607
> Send $5 for a directory of holistic doctors

> Holistic Dental Association
> P.O. Box 5007
> Durango, CO 81301
> Send a S.A.S.E. for a listing of holistic dentists

pH Information

Cleanse and Purify Thyself, Books 1.0 & 2.0 and
The Arise & Shine Cleanse Thyself Program Guide
PH Testing Papers
> (Contact Christine – See Cleanse Information and
> Products)

Alkalize or Die
> Dr. Theodore Baroody
> Eclectic Press
> Waynesville, North Carolina 28786
> (or contact Christine – See Cleanse Information and
> Products)

The Power of Super Foods (Chapter 5, pH information)
> Sam Graci and Harvey Diamond
> Available in your local health food store or call:
> Orange Peel Enterprises, Inc. 1-800-643-1210

Seasonings

Bernard Jensen's Vegetable Seasoning
> See Benard Jensen Int'l. in Cleanse Information and Products

RAW, Dried Vegetable Seasonings (replaces Tomato Power & Vegetable Power)
> Phyllis Avery – Hygeia Enterprises
> P.O. Box 3693
> Vista, CA 92085-3693
> Info: 760-630-8288   Orders Toll Free: 1-877-246-3885

> Tomato Tornado© is great for making tomato soup or tomato juice. It enhances salads, and is a delicious addition to any tomato dish. Try it in tomato sauce. WOW! Ingredients: Dried, ground, raw; tomatoes, onions, parsley, dill, celery, and caraway seed.

> Veggie Valley© is a rich source for your mineral, vitamin, fiber or protein needs. A delicious seasoning for soups, salads, guacamole, entrees, dips and juices. Ingredients: Dried, ground, raw; onions, tomatoes, carrots, spinach, parsley, celery, red & green bell pepper, sweet basil, ground cumin seed and caraway seed.

> Popcorn Pizzazz©, This seasoning can be used for many dishes. Ingredients: Dried, ground, raw; tomatoes, onions, red-& green bell pepper, sweet basil, parsley, and ginger.

> Potato Picnic© is a delightful addition to any potato or vegetable recipe. Selected seasonings are compatible with potatoes. Ingredients: Dried, ground, raw; onions, red and green bell peppers, tomatoes, carrots, spinach, parsley, celery, dill, selected herbs.

Stevia - Wisdom of the Ancients products
> Available at your local health food store or contact Christine Dreher (see Christine's information in Cleanse Information and Products)

Spiritual Transformation and Healing

I recommend the following intensive seminars and private sessions to assist you with the mental, emotional, and spiritual levels of cleansing and healing. I have participated in both of these powerfully healing intensive programs and found them to be truly transformative!

Amanae Intensive Workshops and Private Sessions

Amanae is a hands-on, emotional release, bodywork which opens "doorways" that have been closed by deeply held fear, anger and trauma. Amanae is a journey that takes us back to remembrance and direct experience of the self. The process is about removing barriers from our cellular body and receiving our light and remembering who we really are. There are doorways throughout the body that when opened allow us to access our own light. Once we can access our own light, healing takes place within. Amanae works very much with the heart center. There are many barriers in our hearts and while there are barriers here one cannot receive one's own light or give out in a true form. In Amanae there are certain areas that relate to certain emotions. There are blocked areas in the body that keep us from the experience and remembrance of our divine selves. This work returns us to our natural state as free will beings.

> www.Amanae.org
> Contact Pat Burdy or Christine Day
> 707-463-3354 or 707-463-3356
> patburdy@hotmail.com or christineday3@hotmail.com

Frequencies of Brilliance Certification Program and Private Sessions

The Frequencies of Brilliance 12-Day Certification Program (private sessions also available) is a new level of the multi-dimensional Amanae energy work. This work was founded by Christine Day, along with the original Amanae multi-dimensional bodywork. It in no way replaces the original Amanae work; but it is the next level of teaching and healing. The Frequencies of Brilliance process opens you up to receiving birthing frequencies of Remembrance that activate all cells throughout the body, awakening new areas of the brain, completing DNA re-patterning, and emerging into a new truth and frequency of reality. This process changes the frequencies of the body and prepares us for the transition to higher dimensions of consciousness.

The work is done on the physical body or just above the body, through a series of doorways that hold the purest frequencies of remembrance of Truth. This process allows us to bypass the illusion of the 3rd dimensional reality, allowing us to directly experience the True Light that is here for us to live and be. Awakening occurs on a physical and spiritual level, within your body and within your world. An incredible part of the work involves activating new areas of the brain that have not been accessed in this lifetime. Through a series of special techniques and exercises the muscles of these brain areas are developed and expanded. This certification program initiates you to embody these higher frequencies and to be able to share this work, as a practitioner with others in private sessions.

www.FrequenciesofBrilliance.org
Contact Christine Day or Pat Burdy
707-463-3356 or 707-463-3354
christineday3@hotmail.com or patburdy@hotmail.com

Resources and References